AUDUBON NATURE YEARBOOK 1987

AUDUBON NATURE

1987 YEARBOOK

LES LINE, EDITOR

Grolier Books, New York

Distributed to the trade by Stackpole Books, Harrisburg, Pennsylvania

COVER PHOTO: MARTIN W. GROSNICK
TITLE PAGE PHOTO: TIM FITZHARRIS

Published by

Grolier Books
800 North Pearl Street
Latham, NY 12204

Distributed to the trade by

Stackpole Books
Cameron and Kelker Streets
Harrisburg, PA 17105

Produced by Soderstrom Publishing Group Inc.
Book design by Nai Chang
Typography by Rochester Mono/Headliners

ISBN 0-943822-97-1
ISSN 0891-981X

Manufactured in the United States of America

CONTENTS

WILD PLANTS AND MAN

SPECIAL PLACES

THE ARTIST AND NATURE

PREFACE

The Audubon Magazine, our founding editor George Bird Grinnell wrote a century ago, "will deal with bird life and other natural history, and discuss the general economic problems of animal life in relation to agriculture and human welfare. It will aim to be practical, instructive, and helpful; but it will never be prosy. With inspiration drawn from the great book of nature, how can its pages have other than variety, freshness and charm?"

February 1887. Posted to a roll of 20,000 members of the fledgling Audubon Society in some 400 towns was Volume 1, Number 1, of *The Audubon Magazine,* a slim 24 pages and a trim 7 by 10 inches in size, its cover appropriately decorated with an engraving of the great frontier birdman John James Audubon. The annual subscription price, 50 cents. A single copy, 6 cents. Within, one found a rather fanciful account of Audubon's early years (he was notorious for embellishing his life's story); a profile of a favorite bird, the Baltimore oriole, in the colorful natural history style of the times; a fable for young readers; advertisements for mincemeat, rum calf's-foot jelly, and blackberry brandy from a purveyor of table delicacies, and for high-lace shoes at $4 a pair. And an essay, "Woman's Heartlessness," by the New England poet Celia Thaxter. The target of her ire was the high fashion of wearing the feathers and skins of birds, and her fervor is felt across the decades:

"One lady said to me, 'I think there is a great deal of sentiment wasted on the birds. There are so many of them, they will never be missed, any more than mosquitoes. I shall put birds on my new bonnet' . . . And she went her way, a charnel house of beaks and claws and bones and feathers and glass eyes upon her fatuous head."

Although there were other matters of concern, such as the popular and destructive hobby of collecting birds' nests and their eggs, it was this slaughter of birds for the millinery trade—not only the egrets and herons whose flowing nuptial plumes were most prized by hatmakers, but terns and gulls and even small songbirds—that had led to the founding of the Audubon movement a year earlier. The scope of the traffic is difficult to grasp in this enlightened age: One New York firm had a contract to supply 40,000 skins of American birds to a Paris couturier, another 200,000 skins in its warehouse; wings and breasts of gulls brought poachers $12 for a dozen pieces.

Most surprisingly, the impetus for an organized bird-protection movement in America came not from the ornithological community, which declined to soil its scientific hands in the name of activism—even though the subjects of its study were fast being obliterated—but from a sportsman. He was George Bird Grinnell, editor of the weekly out-of-doors newspaper-magazine *Forest & Stream.* Grinnell had grown up in Audubon Park, the birdman's former estate on the Hudson River in upper Manhattan. The property had been subdivided to ease the tremendous debt left to his widow and sons when the artist died in 1851, but the land was still quite wild, especially to an exploring child, with great white pines along the river, chestnuts, oaks, and tulip trees, a tumbling brook. Migrating passenger pigeons could be shot from the roof of the Grinnell house. And there was Grandma Audubon, the birdman's long-suffering wife Lucy, to inspire a budding naturalist.

In his front-page editorials in *Forest & Stream,* Grinnell had vigorously defended Yellowstone park, lobbied for the creation of a forest preserve in New York's Adirondack wilds, assailed market-hunters and condemned unsportsmanlike behavior, worried over the decimation of big-game herds. In a book review in those newsprint pages, he was critical of the hunting tales of Theodore Roosevelt, who stormed into Grinnell's office demanding an explanation. The editor and the future President became companions, founding the Boone and Crockett Club, collaborating on book projects. And clearly, the seeds of Teddy Roosevelt's future conservation achievements were sown in their friendship.

But the Grinnell editorial that changed the course of conservation history dealt with more fragile life-forms than bison and bears, deer and elk. The date was February 11, 1888. "Very slowly the public are awakening to see that the fashion of wearing the feathers and skins of birds is abominable," Grinnell wrote. "How can we best go to work to combat this great and growing evil?" And he had an answer ready:

"In the first half of this century there lived a man who did more to teach Americans about birds of their own land than any other who ever lived. His beautiful and spirited paintings and his charming and tender accounts of the habits of his favorites have made him immortal, and have inspired his countrymen with an ardent love for birds. This land which produced the painter-naturalist John James Audubon will not willingly see the beautiful forms he loved so well exterminated.

"We propose the formation of an association for the protection of wild birds and their eggs, which shall be called The Audubon Society... The objects for which it is formed... shall be to prevent, so far as possible, (1) the killing of any wild birds not used for food, (2) the destruction of nests or eggs of any wild bird, and (3) the wearing of feathers as ornaments or trimming for dress... Those who are willing to aid us in our labors are urged to establish local societies for work in their own neighborhoods."

And then a year later, from the editorial offices of Forest and Stream Publishing Company, came this new journal, *The Audubon Magazine,* its avowed purpose "to spread the Audubon movement as widely as possible, and in every way to foster its growth." For two years it was dispatched monthly to the fast-growing ranks of the Audubon Society—50,000 members by 1888. And then publication abruptly ceased. It is true that Grinnell was discouraged by the general public's apathy toward the cause of bird preservation, but he and his small staff were in fact overwhelmed by success, by the labor and cost of publishing two magazines.

But though the national movement faltered with the disappearance of its voice, local Audubon Societies begat state Audubon Societies, and in 1899 the noted ornithologist Frank M. Chapman picked up the movement's fallen editorial banner with a magazine that he called *Bird-Lore.* Not many years later a National Association of Audubon Societies (today's National Audubon Society) was incorporated. Grinnell applauded and urged its leaders to "have as a part of its work the protection of birds, the protection of mammals, the protection of forests, and generally, so far as possible, the protection of the natural things of the land." In 1941 the Society's journal became, once again, *Audubon Magazine.* And the rest, as they say, is history.

Those of us who have followed in George Bird Grinnell's editorial footsteps have not deviated from the path he so eloquently laid out one hundred years ago. Some of the issues have changed. Who, in 1887, would have imagined, in his worst nightmare, toxic chemicals or acid rain threatening the natural and human environment? And, of course, the despicable traffic in bird feathers was halted long ago, although it has its recent counterpart in the slaughter of spotted cats for fur coats and alligators for shoes. But economic conflicts remain at the root of all wildlife conservation problems, and those conflicts become increasingly more difficult to resolve. As for inspiration, we continue to draw from the great book of nature, with variety, freshness, and charm. The proof is in the twenty-four articles in this first *Audubon Nature Yearbook*—the first, we anticipate, of many. For the finest writing, photography, and art of their kind are to be found in the pages of this century-old magazine, and they deserve both a wider distribution and the permanence of a hard cover. Enjoy, as I have enjoyed editing these stories the second time around.

Les Line

I
MOSTLY MAMMALS

TALES OF A DOUR DOORMAT

TEXT BY JOHN MADSON · PHOTOGRAPHY BY ROBERT P. CARR

Apart from the rather singular name, I remember John Stopsack for several things.

There was his homesite at the foot of Ocheyedan Mound, a great kame of sand and gravel that had been dumped by a river of meltwater pouring from a retreating glacier. This vast pile of Pleistocene rubbish was overlain with a blanket of rich loam and prairie grasses and dominated the farmscapes below. At 1,675 feet above sea level it was then regarded as the highest point in Iowa. Stopsack didn't farm the Mound, explaining that it was strong on drainage but weak on level plowground, and the place was largely relegated to the retirement of Old Rich, the venerable workhorse that dominated the summit of Ocheyedan Mound for twenty-six years, off and on. Tail and mane streaming in the wind, he was a landmark for miles. It was about as close to heaven as an Iowa horse could get. Especially in flytime.

Old Rich didn't have the Mound to himself. Such a place is too special to be exclusive, and the horse shared tenancy with several badgers in a placid arrangement that never did include John Stopsack. On the contrary, John and those badgers had a running feud that often broke into open conflict—such as the memorable time he tried to crash a badger sex orgy.

It happened one September night during the badger mating season when a particularly wild party up on the Mound was keeping Stopsack awake.

"You never heard such squealing and squalling and carrying on," he told me. "Fighting and raising hell up there. Nobody could sleep. Along in the middle of the night I had enough of it. Got dressed and grabbed a club and clumb the hill to join in. If them badgers wanted fight, I'd give 'em fight! I was as mad as they were—or thought I was. Well, I got in one lick before they run me right back down the hill again. Let me tell you, don't *never* mess around with a bunch of horny badgers!"

Beyond the touch of comic opera in this, it must have really been something up there on that great mound in the darkness. It all happened high on the roof of the prairie, an island in time rising from a sea of cash grain, one of the old places being defended against infidels by its ancient keepers. An enraged badger is forbidding enough by noon—what must several look like in the midwatches of night, grizzled coats faintly luminous under a gibbous moon that distorts their size and intensifies the ferocity of their shambling, hissing attacks? It was a vignette of pure wildness; no wonder John Stopsack gave it back to the badgers.

Badgers and places like Ocheyedan Mound belong together. Both are anachronisms—survivors of the wild grassland biomes that once covered much of the western two-thirds of the United States and Canada. As grassland originals, badgers are most at home on prairies and plains although they have extended their range eastward as the hardwood forests have been broken up into fields, pastures, and small woodlots.

Badgers and night belong together, too. I've watched badgers during the day as they prospected about prairie dog towns with apparent indifference to enemies, but there's no doubt that they'd rather be abroad at night. Maybe the hunting is better then, or more fun, or both. The coyote feels much the same, preferring to pursue his affairs under the moon than the sun. And since badgers and coyotes share many tastes (but not, usually, a taste for each other), it was probably inevitable that they got together in some way.

The famous badger-coyote hunting alliance must be the coyote's idea, because the badger sure doesn't get much out of it. A coyote attends a badger in much the same way it might hang around an elk that's pawing in snow and flushing mice in the process. As the badger digs into ground squirrel burrows, prairie dog holes, or nests of packrats, an alert coyote may stand ready for any prey that gets past the badger and breaks into the open. It's been said that the coyote pays his own way by forcing rodents to den up so that the badger can dig them out—but that doesn't make a lot of sense. A badger hunts and digs just fine without any tactical support from a coyote.

black sideburns and white striping. A badger, a big one, on the hunt. It came up out of the hole quickly, trailed along the ground for a couple of yards, and froze. Its attention was riveted by something underground; the frenzied digging was resumed, and the badger vanished almost instantly. When the digging stopped this time, however, several minutes passed before the badger emerged. It looked around, muzzle high and tasting the air, then sat back and deliberately cleaned its front feet before ambling off in that pigeon-toed, head-swinging way that has always reminded me of a miniature grizzly. Three prospect holes had been dug in a direct line, all plumbing some part of a Richardson's ground squirrel's burrow, and each a bit deeper than the one before. The head and tail of the luckless resident lay at the bottom of the third pit. The badger had known just what to do, and just where to do it.

That happened early on a bright summer day. The badger was highly visible in an open pasture in closely settled farm country, yet didn't give the impression of being especially wary. Rather, it left the impression that there wasn't much of anything in that neighborhood that couldn't be easily handled.

Now, all my life I've been hearing about farm dogs that kill badgers. I don't give such reports the lie, but I'm inclined to assign them to the same category as those wonder-working bird dogs that always seem to have died or been sold out of state. All I know is that it would take a mighty dedicated dog to kill a badger—far more dedicated than the typical yard dog is likely to be. An old badger's neck, shoulders, and legs are massively thewed, with claws and dentition that are nothing short of awesome. While a big dog is trying to chew through the tough, loose skin and thick muscle that protects vital parts, the badger will be cutting him deep, long, wide, and consecutive, as they say. Add to this that special quality of agile strength that's the hallmark of the weasel tribe and you have a creature that can easily whip twice his weight in common dogs.

In H. Hediger's classic *Wild Animals in Captivity,* the famed director of the Basle Zoological Gardens cited the badger and Tasmanian devil as the two most notorious cage-breakers in zoos. He was probably speaking of the European badger, *Meles meles,* but the same applies to our American species, *Taxidea taxus.*

The badger cage in our conservation department's traveling wildlife exhibit was barred with 5/16-inch rods of cold-rolled steel spaced two inches apart and welded at top and bottom. Its occupant was an old,

In a general sense, predators have to be better than their prey at doing what the prey does best. Part of the time, anyway. The goshawk may out-fly a ruffed grouse, the otter may out-swim a squawfish—and the badger can out-dig almost anything. Technically, it's a fossorial mustelid—a powerful digging weasel that is superbly designed for moving much soil in little time, literally sinking out of sight under a geyser of flying dirt.

I once came over a hilltop in a prairie pasture and was startled by such a soil geyser not far down the slope. There was no sign of its cause—just that column of dirt shooting five feet into the air. As I lay down to watch, the geyser ceased, and out of the hole popped the distinctive broad, pointed head with large, and particularly disenchanted male that yearned for more open horizons—and had the wherewithal to do something about it. One day he snapped the weld on a cage bar, bent it up, and was working on the next one when he was discovered. The exhibit supervisor pried the bar back into place. The badger then broke the bar off. The disgusted supervisor closed the outer cage cover and went home.

During the night the badger attacked the expanded steel flooring of the cage, which was welded on all sides. He tore one of the welds and opened a six-inch gap in the edge of the cage floor and was on the verge of busting out of the joint when the supervisor got there. Enough was enough. The crusty old boar was turned loose and replaced with a younger, more tractable animal.

Not long before that, some new outdoor cages with concrete floors were being built at the state game farm. A big boar badger was released into a cage whose flooring had been poured late the afternoon before. The concrete had not cured but had set enough to support a man. It was surely badger-proof, right? Wrong. The badger dug through the green concrete, tore through the fox-wire netting beneath it, and made his getaway. Verily, that was an era of heroic badgers....

But formidable as he is, the badger brings a certain air of comic relief to his grim daily affairs. For one thing, he's put together funny—a bowlegged, pigeon-toed doormat that sweeps the ground with its trailing end. He also has a dour quality of the sort usually associated with the Scots. Walt Disney, with an unerring eye for anthropomorphism, had this in mind when he created the arch-conservative Angus MacBadger in the Disney version of "Wind in the Willows." And when someone like the dour Angus Mac-Badger gets an itch under his kilts, it can be pretty good slapstick.

My old friend W. Glenn Titus was once photographing a black-footed ferret in a South Dakota prairie dog town when he noticed a large badger stalking the ferret. Flat to the ground, stealthily closing on the busy ferret, the badger was suddenly smitten with an acute flea problem. Every few yards he would stop, scratch himself furiously, and then resume his stalk. It didn't come off, of course. You can't scratch and sneak at the same time and do either properly. The ferret ducked into a burrow, the badger went doormatting grumpily into the sunrise—stopping now and then to scratch—and Glenn was left with no film record of the event. "It might have been wonderful footage if I'd had a wide-angle lens," he says wistfully, "but

what the heck. I was laughing too hard to get it, anyway."

There are times when the badger has the last laugh. A coyote and badger were seen hunting together in New Mexico when the coyote decided to liven things up with some badger-baiting. As the badger began to dig, the songdog would dart in, nip him on the rump, and dodge nimbly away from the badger's slashing response. This grumbling badger would then resume digging, only to be bitten again. This went on until the badger had finally gotten the hole deep enough to disappear into—and turn around in. It must have been a young coyote, or one with a hopeless case of the simples. Anyway, it stuck its head into the burrow to see what the badger was up to. When the coyote finally pried its face out of those awful jaws, it had lost all interest in further badgering.

The folklore of the prairies is rich with such stories, but there are gaps in badger life history that science still hasn't bridged. And although there have been some excellent recent studies of local badger populations there is little ecological perspective of the North American population as a whole.

The expansion of the badger's range during recent times reveals an unusual quality: a predator not only highly specialized in form and function, but remarkably adaptable as well. The badger is managing to fit in. There are always clashes with man, of course. Now and then a badger develops a taste for poultry and may even kill lambs, although in Colorado this was found to occur only when the lambs had gotten into holes from which they couldn't escape. A sheepman can get bitter about things like that—but not nearly as bitter as the cattleman whose livestock break legs in badger diggings.

A rancher friend west of Fort Pierre, South Dakota, had an interesting way of looking at this. He was a traditionalist who savored the old things: he liked beefsteak fried well-done, had more horses than he'd ever need, kept his original log outbuildings and corrals, and supported a couple of prairie dog towns and resident badgers. I asked him if those diggers threatened his beloved horses.

"Well, I ain't denying that a horse can bust a leg in a badger hole," he replied, "but I ain't had it happen in fifty years, and I've ridden in some mighty dug-up country. If a cowhorse of mine can't see a badger hole in time to dodge it, he oughta have his leg broke—and I oughta have my neck broke for keepin' a horse that dumb. Besides, what would a west-river spread be without some sod poodles and a badger or two?"

What, indeed?

"As grassland originals, badgers are most at home on prairies and plains although they have extended their range eastward as the hardwood forests have been broken up into fields, pastures, and small woodlots."

13

YOU'LL NEVER SEE A

Unless you are luckier than many biologists who have studied this wilderness recluse

One day some years ago I topped a knoll in a wild and remote region of central California. As I came over the ridge and looked down into a rocky little valley interspersed with thickets and grassy openings, a brownish long-legged cat with a stubby tail bounded away in a loping run. This was the first bobcat I had ever seen in the wild, and since then, in a quarter of a century of tramping the outdoors from lowland swamp to mountaintop, I have not seen another.

Seeing even one bobcat is above the average. Most Americans—campers, hikers, birdwatchers, and hunters included—never even catch a glimpse of these elusive native cats. One wildlife scientist who earned his doctorate studying the animal told me that in twenty-five years of tramping the hills of Wyoming he had seen bobcats without the aid of dogs only four times. Another field biologist who has lived in Missouri and Florida and who studies the bobcat has spotted only one.

One reason that sightings are so infrequent is that the bobcat, like most felines, is nocturnal, so during the day it lurks in the shadows, lying motionless, watching as humans plod past, sometimes within feet of the rocks or brush pile where it is hiding. "Behavior of the bobcat is extremely difficult to study in the wild," biologist Douglas M. Crowe of the Wyoming Game and Fish Department, an authority on bobcats, told me. "It is solitary, nocturnal, and thinly spaced over its range."

Perhaps as long as men have known the bobcat, they have respected its fighting ability. The rough and tumble frontier fighter who boasted he could lick his weight in wildcats would have been best advised not to put it to the test because the bobcat, young or old, is all spitfire and lightning. "Even a little bobkitten," a professional trapper once told me, "is just meaner than strychnine. I don't think there's anything'll raise hell with you quicker than a little bobcat, unless it's a big one."

Joe Van Wormer wrote, in his book *The World of the Bobcat,* "I have never seen one that had a look of fear in its eyes, even when caught in a steel trap." Wildlife officers occasionally are called upon to release trapped bobcats, caught illegally. Stanley P. Young, a legendary government trapper, once wrote,

BOBCAT

TEXT BY GEORGE LAYCOCK · PHOTOGRAPHY BY GLENN D. CHAMBERS

Bobcat females raise one litter of kittens a year. The kittens are on a meat diet by June and instinctively try to kill prey animals.

"Attempting to remove a live adult bobcat from a trap is a never-to-be-forgotten experience." One state worker explained that it takes two men to hold one down with a pole while it is released.

Another wildlife professional, a federal officer, once told me, "The bobcat has one foot in the trap and three waiting for you, so I carry a six-foot length of steel pipe with a flexible wire run through it to make a loop that I can slip over the cat's head. That way I can hold him down with the pipe across him long enough to release his foot."

Besides being a fierce fighter, the bobcat is versatile and adaptable. This smallest of North American wildcats occupies a range reaching from coast to coast and from Mexico into southern Canada. From sea level to 6,000 feet, and sometimes beyond, the bobcat, *Lynx rufus,* pads silently through a wide variety of countryside. It thrives in the swamps of the southeastern states, including the Everglades. It is at home in the hardwood

forests of the eastern mountains, the coniferous forests of the West, the rocky canyons and river bottoms of range country, and in the dry desert of the Southwest. The bobcat survives anywhere it can find sufficient prey and terrain with plentiful hiding places.

The one place the bobcat does not thrive is where man has transformed the land—the miles and miles of America given over to towns, factories, and farms. Delaware considers the animal gone now, while across Ohio, Indiana, and Illinois, people gathered in crossroads stores, at sportsmen's clubs, or meetings of biologists debate about whether the cat has disappeared there, too. In the rugged hills of southern Ohio, where I live, I find it difficult to accept the idea that the bobcat is gone, perhaps because I do not *want* it to be gone. I am encouraged by the knowledge that the bobcat, recluse that it is, would not publicly announce its going, so no one can insist with certainty that it has vanished.

When grown, bobcats are three feet long, stand fifteen to eighteen inches high, and weigh from fifteen to twenty-five pounds. Sometimes there are larger individuals, but almost never does one weigh more than forty pounds. Females are about 25 percent smaller than males. Bobcats have long legs but short tails—only six inches long. The bobcat's winter coat is more grayish in color than the black-spotted rufous fur it wears in summer. It has a distinctive ruff or sidewhiskers on its face and tufts of antennae-like hair on the points of its ears. Tests have shown that captive bobcats lose some of their keen hearing if these hairs are snipped off.

In the northern areas of its range, the bobcat is larger and darker than it is in the south, and its fur is more dense and therefore more valuable to the fur trade. In its northern ranges, it also gives way to the larger Canada lynx. One certain way to tell them apart, aside from the variation in size, is by the tail. The bobcat has a black bar on the upper surface of the tail and the tip is white, but the tail of the Canada lynx has an all-black tip.

Where they prevail, bobcats are spread thinly upon the land. Wildlife biologist Theodore N. Bailey of the Idaho Cooperative Wildlife Research Unit spent three years studying these predators along the Snake River in southeastern Idaho. With the aid of telemetry he was able to define the home ranges of individual male and female bobcats. Females, he found, maintain exclusive territories in relation to other females, while areas used by the males sometimes overlap those of the females. Not surprising, since the ranges of the males he studied were more than twice as large as those of the females.

Solitary hunters, the cats use their scent-marking techniques to divide the available space among themselves and maintain their territorial boundaries. As a bobcat makes its rounds through the night or in the half-light of dusk or dawn, it uses feces, urine, and a viscous yellowish excretion from its anal gland to mark earth, rocks, bushes, or snow with a label that signals a neighboring cat to keep its distance. For if bobcats, with their razor-edged teeth, sharp claws, and sour dispositions, were to defend their territories by physical combat, their fights would threaten the survival of the species.

Under severe pressures, however, adult bobcats sometimes come together and live in apparent harmony, seeming to set aside the ancient social structure by common consent. Bailey, during his study of the social organization of a bobcat population in the rugged hills of southeastern Idaho, with its craters, caves, and lava flows, once observed a gathering of bobcats. Writing in the *Journal of Wildlife Management,* he reported, "A most unusual association of adult bobcats took place during a period of inclement weather and general rabbit scarcity in the winter of 1971–72." For more than a month that winter the land lay beneath deep snow, swept by bitter winds and held in the grip of subzero temperatures. Drifting snow sealed off ledges and thickets where the cats normally took refuge. One exception was a mound of large boulders offering numerous caverns where a bobcat could escape wind and snow and also live close to a supply of the scarce rabbits.

Bailey discovered four bobcats, two males and two females, taking refuge there. They sometimes slept within six or seven feet of each other. Even then, however, they kept their distance from each other and hunted and dined alone. For two weeks they stayed there, until the weather moderated and they could return to their own hunting grounds.

For years, government predator-control agents collected the stomach contents from bobcats they killed and shipped them off for analysis in the laboratories of the U.S. Fish and Wildlife Service. As the contents were identified, the list of foods consumed by the cats grew. The bobcat is an opportunist, but when given a choice it leans heavily on rabbits. It also includes tree squirrels, ground squirrels, and prairie dogs in its diet and looks upon porcupines as edible. It even swallows porcupine quills, which appear to pass through its system with no great harm. But if it gets too many quills stuck in its face and lips it cannot eat and will die of starvation.

Other foods commonly taken by bobcats include songbirds and grouse, rats, mice of any variety, grasshoppers, beetles, and reptiles, including rattlesnakes. Bobcats also are known to consume grapes from cultivated vineyards, as well as the fruit of the prickly-pear cactus.

Bobcats are not limited to small and easily taken prey. They are able to kill young antelope and deer, and on occasion adult deer as

Solitary and nocturnal, bobcats usually stalk close enough to take prey in one or two bounding leaps, rather than engaging in long chases.

17

well. This is most frequently accomplished when the deer is bedded down, unaware that it is being stalked. The cat inches carefully toward it, then bounds forward and lands on the deer's neck and shoulders. If the bobcat's teeth reach the deer's spine, the deer may be killed quickly, but if the deer is large and strong it may leap up, with the bobcat still on its back, and bound through the forest trying to shake the cat off. With luck, it may scrape its attacker off against a low branch. But more probably the bobcat will ride the deer to earth, biting deeper and deeper into its neck.

Depending on opportunities and pressures, bobcats may eat carrion. In northern states they are said to feed on the remains of deer that died of starvation or were left in the woods during the hunting season. While engaged in bobcat research in northern Michigan, Albert W. Erickson tracked cats to and from the carcasses of deer. "The cat is an inherently lazy creature," he said, "but it grows fat in winter, wandering from carcass to carcass."

I heard another version of the cat's preferences, however, in Utah, where I talked with Orson Carter, who for sixty-five years worked as a professional trapper, first for the Fish and Wildlife Service, and later for stockmen who felt their sheep and cattle threatened by predators. "A cat likes its meat fresh and bloody," he told me. "Let it get a few days old and dry out a little and you couldn't get him to eat it if you poked it down him with a stick."

Sheep ranchers in particular have cursed bobcats, sometimes with good cause. In the past ranchers frequently chose rocky canyons for lambing, where the ewes and newborns would be protected from the wind. Such places are often home base for bobcats, and flocks driven into the canyon overwhelm the predator with temptation. The bobcat is less of a threat to domestic livestock today because many farmers provide special lambing barns for their stock.

The female bobcat raises one litter of kittens a year. As spring approaches and she is heavy with young she searches out a spot among tumbled boulders at the base of a canyon wall or crawls back beneath the up-turned roots of a wind-downed tree. In less rugged terrain she may find a hollow log or even an abandoned building in which to make her nest. During the last weeks of her pregnancy she spends most of the daylight hours in her hiding place, coming out to hunt at night. And when spring comes she gives birth to her kittens, fur-covered and helpless. Commonly there are two or three young in the litter. For their first nine days the kittens live in darkness, their eyes sealed.

Now the mother must hunt for her family—the male is long gone—and the little spotted kittens grow steadily more demanding. By June the kittens are on a meat diet, and although the female weans them, she does not abandon them, for first they must learn the rudiments of survival in the wild. Even when very young and unskilled, they instinctively try to kill. Van Wormer tells of a litter of bobcats born in captivity that were still on a milk diet when a partly grown white rabbit was placed among them to test their reaction. Though the kittens had never seen such an animal before, one of them pounced and took a grip on the back of the rabbit's neck, and the rabbit had to be rescued.

In the early summer the newly weaned kittens begin following their mother on her nightly hunts. The hunt is not a careless expenditure of energy. She moves slowly and methodically, a spotted shadow in the darkness. Her feet touch the ground gently and noiselessly. She is a thorough hunter, constantly alert for signs of prey, especially the rabbit, which is also feeding at this hour. In the dark the pupils of her eyes enlarge to cover most of the eyeball and enable her to see form and movement. If you have watched a domestic cat stalking a bird, you have witnessed the bobcat's technique in stalking a rabbit. The unsuspecting rabbit munches grass, stopping occasionally to lift its head and twitch its nose before resuming its meal. The cat, crouched low to the ground, stretches out, plants its feet, and inches forward, eyes riveted on its intended prey. When the cat is close enough she makes one or two bounding leaps, and the hunt is over quickly, whether the cat is successful or not. The bobcat is not equipped for long or swift pursuit and does not waste energy attempting to run down missed prey. Instead it goes off in search of another victim, and this is the lesson the young cat must learn.

Many of them learn it too late. As autumn comes and the adult cats go into the breeding season again, the young, their training ended, are abandoned by the mother. The young cats now wander the land, often staying together into the winter. This is a critical time in their lives, the test of their ability to survive. "There is normally a high mortality rate among juveniles," Crowe says. "In years when there is a high population of cottontail rabbits, survival among juvenile bobcats will be high, maybe as high as seventy percent. But when rabbit populations are low, the survival of young cats may fall to zero."

Every bobcat's life is structured by its relation to all the other bobcats in the area. They are, as Crowe says, "highly social and extremely territorial." Researchers do not yet know whether the size of a cat's territory changes with the abundance or scarcity of food and whether more bobcats can live closer together if food supplies permit. Older animals, occupying ranges undisturbed by hunting and trapping, are the most successful hunters. They also may be the most successful parents. Their strength lies in the fact that they are already in control of territories that are defined, marked, and therefore off limits to other bobcats. In such areas, where there is minimum turnover, newly weaned cats must stake out their territories farther and farther from where they learned to hunt. When they do find a territory large enough to feed them and free of the scents of other bobcats, they may have gone beyond the best hunting grounds. This, coupled with their youthful ineptitude, reduces their chance of survival through the cold winter months.

Crowe also studied the age at which bobcats first go into the breeding population. Males, he found, do not produce sperm the first year of their lives, but females may breed that first year. However, if a female fails to breed by February and is impregnated later, her young may arrive late in the spring, bringing them to autumn less experienced than they might have been, and this further reduces their chance of surviving the winter. Little is known about how successful these young females are in producing young to supplement the population.

Especially in the northern parts of its range, the bobcat, like many other animals, may hole up and wait out the severe storms. Travel is difficult for it in deep snow, and the demands on its energy can exceed the gains.

Country people may awaken on a winter night to the courting serenade of bobcats in a distant woods or canyon. The "caterwauling" resembles the snarling, hissing, squalling, deep-throated growling, and high-pitched squeals of the domestic cat in the hour of mating—but with the volume turned up. The naturalist and teacher Edmund C. Jaeger was once awakened by this serenade in the middle of night while camping in the Southwest. "Luckily it was moonlight," Jaeger wrote, "and I was able to see the animals almost perfectly. The female most of the time lay crouched upon the ground, while the big male, which must have weighed twenty pounds, walked menacingly around her. Sometimes they both sat upright facing each other. The loud and ludicrous serenade was kept up for almost an

Although bobcats prey mainly on rabbits and other small animals, they can kill adult deer. The bobcat stalks a bedded deer, pounces on the neck and shoulders, and bites into the spine.

hour, and it ended with a dual climax of discordant, frightening squalls as mating took place." Mating accomplished, the cats separate, and in sixty-three to seventy days the female bears her new kittens. This continues year after year as long as she lives, which may be twelve to fifteen years.

On occasion the discoverer of a family of bobcat kittens has yielded to the temptation to take them for pets—and usually lived to regret it. When the bobcat was without legal protection, as was the case in many states until recently, it could be kept without a special permit from the state wildlife agency. These live-in arrangements rarely succeeded because almost invariably the semi-domesticated bobcat is antagonistic toward everyone except the person or family to which it "belongs." A bobcat owner may tolerate having his "pet" climb the draperies and claw the stuffing out of his furniture. But when the cat goes for the throat of a visitor—a not unlikely occurrence—the owner is ready to present his animal to the nearest zoo. And the zoo won't want to take it either, because its staff knows the cat probably will die soon and tragically. Deprived of familiar surroundings and people, captive-reared cats usually will refuse to eat and die of starvation.

There is a fraternity of hunters who keep hounds for running down bobcats. Commonly the cat seeks refuge in a tree, and the hunters can tell by the howling of their dogs when this occurs. The dogs leap around the trunk of the tree, holding the cat at bay until the owners arrive to shoot it. G. W. Evans, once a New Mexico state senator, claims he encountered a bobcat his hounds never could catch. He could not understand why his normally successful hounds consistently lost its trail. He learned the answer one day when the trail led into country so rough that his horse could no longer follow. He turned up a spur trail to come out ahead of the hounds, and standing on a point, he could see the action.

The cat, well ahead of the hounds, ran across the canyon. While the hounds still bayed in the distance, it ran up a large pine tree and came right down again. Then it doubled back the way it had come. As the hounds drew close to the tree their excited baying echoed through the canyon. Meanwhile the cat, about fifty yards from the tree, turned sharply and slipped from sight into the next canyon. This was the last glimpse Evans had of the animal. His hounds raced to the empty tree, peered into its bushy top, and announced with full confidence that the cat was finally treed. Evans was so impressed with the cat's behavior that he called off the hounds.

From the earliest days of human presence on this continent the large wild predators have been considered man's enemies. Bears, cougars, wolves, eagles, hawks—all had to go. Massachusetts offered a bobcat bounty as early as 1727, and other states followed. In this atmosphere boys grew to manhood convinced that killing bobcats was a social responsibility, an economic opportunity, and an avenue to peer approval. The fact that the bobcat survived at all stands as a tribute to its ability to hide and its capacity to adapt to changing conditions.

For most of these years, however, the bobcat's economic value was almost nil. Its fur generally was considered inferior and sometimes so low in price that hunters and trappers did not even bother to skin the cats they killed. There were years when the fur might bring a couple of dollars, and sometimes only fifty cents. Seven to ten dollars was a good price prior to 1967. Then the American bobcat found itself in demand as laws were passed to protect the world's large spotted cats. With the skins of leopards and cheetahs no longer readily available, the fur industry developed a new respect for the bobcat. Bobcat fur prices were up to twenty dollars by the winter of 1966–67. And by the 1975–76 season top-quality northern bobcat pelts, referred to in the fur trade as lynx cat, were commanding $300 to $400 each.

The effect of such news was predictable. Old hunters, who had spat on the ground when bobcat furs were mentioned, dug out rusted traps and went back into business, while new weekend trappers roared into the hills on snowmobiles. In Idaho, two enterprising high school boys moved into the wilds of the Salmon River country and chartered a jet boat. They made three weekend trips from Pittsburg Landing into wild country where nobody else had trapped, and they cleared $2,000 on bobcat furs alone.

In this atmosphere the bobcat didn't stand a chance. One reason is that it is one of the world's easiest animals to trap. As it hunts, the bobcat is constantly alert for signs of motion. Trappers have learned to suspend a moving object above their hidden traps—pieces of rabbit fur, wings of a raven, or even a rag or aluminum plate to swing in the breeze. The sharp-eyed cat can spot the movement from across a canyon. Unsuspecting, it stalks and leaps—landing on the pan of the waiting trap.

The high value of the furs brought the bobcat sudden recognition in state legislatures, especially throughout the West. States that had always considered the cat a pest and a predator undeserving of legal protection were now changing. Legislatures began reclassifying the bobcat either as furbearer or game animal, permitting wildlife agencies to give it the protection of closed seasons at least part of the year. The deadly swinging baits used over traps became widely illegal.

Then in 1975 the United States became a party to the Convention on International Trade in Endangered Species of Wild Fauna and Flora, a treaty aimed at banning trade in endangered wildlife and controlling trade in many other species. As a result, the United States was required to establish an Endangered Species Scientific Authority. This interagency body is obligated to ban exports of nonendangered animals or plants unless the states in which they originate can offer evidence that taking them will not deplete populations unduly. State agencies scrambled for proof that their bobcats could be taken safely, and eventually many states were assigned quotas.

The Fish and Wildlife Service claimed there might be as many as a million bobcats, and under considerable pressure from the states it proposed to ask the international treaty body to remove the bobcat from any export restrictions. But the backlash from conservationists was such that the service withdrew the proposal. And though various states now limit or prohibit the taking of bobcats, the bobcat is still considered by many to be in a state of siege.

Some wildlife biologists, however, consider the health of the cat's habitat to be more critical to its survival than the pressure on it created by the international demand for its fur. And these authorities warn that only if we leave the bobcat enough wilderness space for hunting and hiding will it be secure in the years ahead.

Adult bobcats usually weigh fifteen to twenty-five pounds, rarely weighing forty pounds. The "bobbed" tail is about six inches long.

GAMES OTTERS PLAY

TEXT BY GEORGE LAYCOCK · PHOTOGRAPHY BY MICHAEL S. QUINTON

The world so needs to have its spirits lifted that when we find in the wild an animal that seems devoted to games and light-hearted play we rejoice in the discovery. Deep in the Okefenokee Swamp on a summer afternoon I surprised the most persistent of all wild players of games.

On that day the Okefenokee lay beneath a pall of dark clouds, and the subdued light cast water, sky, and moss-draped cypress trees into a moody tapestry. Birds were quiet ahead of the approaching storm. Then I rounded a curve in a boat channel, and well ahead of me I saw a sinuous dark brown animal crawling onto a big cypress knee, where it perched above the swamp's glassy surface.

The animal was about four feet long from its nose to the end of its heavy tail. The head was small and flat, the ears short and scarcely visible. With binoculars, I could see the long stiff whiskers on the sides of its face. The fur was dark-chocolate brown, and the eyes small and black. The creature was a river otter, and it had contours designed to move it through the water with minimum resistance—smooth, uninterrupted flowing lines from nose to tip of tail.

The otter appeared to be carrying a snail, which it placed on top of a cypress knee, balancing it there with gentle touches of its pug nose. Then the snail rolled off and tumbled into the water. The otter's body arched and followed, and there was scarcely a ripple where it pierced the surface. I thought that brief glimpse was the whole show, but the otter reappeared with its recaptured toy. It set the shell up and again let it fall into the water, only to recapture it and bring it back. The game went on as I drifted closer. The otter looked directly toward me, then slipped into the water smoothly and, this time, did not reappear.

The otter is our most primitive land-dwelling carnivore. Fossil finds indicate that there were otters as far back as the Upper Oligocene, perhaps thirty million years ago. In recent times, otters have enjoyed worldwide distribution—there are eighteen species—inhabiting all areas except the severe deserts and the tundra of the Far North. But in all their habitats they are becoming the victims of man's depredations.

In North America, the arrival of European settlers was almost as bad for otters as it was for beavers.

At first, otters were only trapped and shot, but now their home waters have been polluted with silt, pesticides, and other human and chemical wastes. The species whose antics I was enjoying, the North American river otter, *Lutra canadensis,* used to have a range that covered the continent from Alaska on the west to Labrador on the east, stretching down to the deserts of the Southwest and into the tropics of Florida. Today there are hardly any otters left in the great heartland of the United States, and the remaining populations are concentrated in the Northeast, the Southeast, the upper Great Lakes, and the Pacific Northwest.

In recent years, there have been moves—so far unsuccessful—to add the river otter to the U.S. endangered species list. Protection now is confined to listing the otter in Appendix II of the Convention on International Trade in Endangered Species of Fauna and Flora, a listing which means that international trade in its fur is monitored through export and import permits. Also the different states keep records of otters trapped for furs, figures that are tallied each year by the U.S. Fish and Wildlife Service.

During the 1978-79 trapping season, for example, a total of 29,665 otters were taken. During the previous nine years, twenty-nine states reported a total of 183,415 otters harvested, for an average of about 20,000 a year. In the last several seasons, however, the counts have been considerably above this average. Does this indicate that there are more otters, better record-keeping—or both? Critics of the CITES controls contend that, on the contrary, it indicates a lack of control and increased pressures on otter populations. Over recent years otter pelt prices have pushed upward considerably.

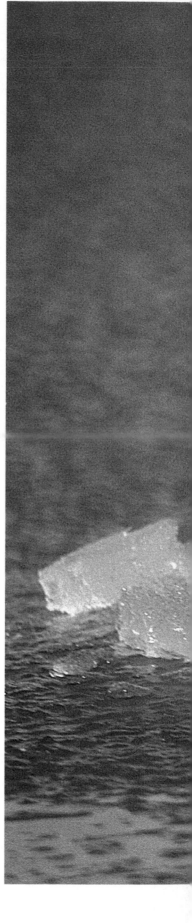

The part of the country where I was watch-ing the otter is, in fact, where the largest numbers of them are trapped. And sup-posedly the largest numbers survive—inventing games to amuse themselves, and those of us lucky enough to see them.

Otters seem to improvise. When swim-ming along in a lake or stream, one may push a leaf or twig ahead of it. Or it may drop a pebble, then chase it through the sparkling water, catching it before it touches bottom, only to bring it to the surface and drop it again. Underwater it may balance a rock or mussel on its head as it swims, or play cat and mouse games with its prey. In captiv-ity it plays games with every moving object and explores all corners and crevices for strings to pull, wires to loosen, latches to open, and new mysteries to solve.

As Ed Park wrote in his book, *The World of the Otter*, "If an otter can't have fun do-ing something, it just simply won't do it." This advanced love of playing sets otters apart from other members of the family Mustelidae. Weasels, skunks, minks, bad-gers, wolverines, martens, fishers, and ferrets seem to us somber and businesslike by com-parison.

Sliding is one of the games otters play best. It is a group sport, seldom enjoyed by lone animals. In summer they may have a mud slide that carries them speeding down a steep slope into the water. They climb up the slope and slide down again and again. This game can be played with entire families fol-lowing each other up the hill and down the slide dozens of times. A cautious or inex-perienced otter may at first hold its front feet out to slow its speed, but before long this caution is abandoned for the "what-the-hell" full-speed approach, with legs held flat against the body to get the full benefit of that wild uninhibited downhill trip. The fin-est otter slides of all are made in the winter on snowbanks above open water. The wet furs of the sliding party and the subfreezing temperatures glaze the run and turn it into a bobsledder's delight. They scoot full-tilt to-ward the water and submerge in the smooth-est imaginable dive. Olympic divers without gold medals!

If otters travel overland on winter snow, they approach the trip as they do everything else, appearing to make a game of it. They mix running with cross-country sledding, al-ternately loping along on their short legs, then sliding on their bellies. They can skid fifteen to twenty feet or more, traveling faster than by running, and perhaps going farther because coasting conserves energy.

But perhaps play actually is vital to the ot-

ter, for if one must play, why play so hard? Behaviorists may tell us that otters do not re-ally play as we play, that they are responding to instinctive drives and that their frenzied play has survival value, sharpening reflexes, building muscles, fine-tuning the ability to maneuver. But who is to say that otters do not have fun?

Given its reputation as the most "fun-loving" of all wild animals, the otter was cer-tain to attract the attention of people seeking unusual company or subjects for study. A fair portion of what we know about the river ot-ter has been learned from captive animals. People who keep otters never forget the ex-perience, and more likely than not, become emotionally tied to the animals. In Florida, a weatherbeaten boatman once told about the otter he had kept and how it loved to dive from the deck and swim around his boat. The boatman's voice broke as he spoke. One evening, another boat pulled up close to his and a man came out onto its deck, pointed a shotgun at his otter, and killed it. This was the end of the story, and it is just as well, be-cause the boatman—who had looked as tough as nails and mean as a pirate—was sob-bing uncontrollably about an otter three years dead.

The otter's tendency to play is sometimes viewed as an indicator of intelligence, and this once gave E. Eugene Good an idea. In 1964, Good, who was then a professor of zo-ology at Ohio State University, was driving along the upper Mississippi River one day when he realized that he had come to the home of "The Otter Man," whose fame was nationwide. On an impulse Good stopped and met Emil E. Liers, who acquired his first pair of young otters in 1928, and who then gave up a career as a professional fur trapper and built a new life around his otters. Liers learned that he could breed them and raise them in captivity. At one time he had thirty-five otters in pens and romping around his yard. His otters, as devoted to Liers as he was to them, accompanied him on his travels. They even learned to retrieve ducks during the hunting season, performing the task far more skillfully than the finest dogs Liers ever owned. Liers eventually spent much of his time traveling with a pair of his otters and lecturing to school groups and organizations. He happily showed the professor from Ohio his animals and talked at length about their care and their special qualities.

Good was searching for an animal he and his graduate students could use in experi-ments to test the learning abilities of ani-mals, and although the head of his de-partment urged him to use mites, Good

dismissed the idea out of hand: "What could you teach a mite?" Otters held far greater appeal, and Liers directed the professor to an automobile dealer in Kansas City known to have a pair of otters for sale. The $500 price was considered reasonable, and eventually Good received word that his otters were waiting at the Columbus airport. Each animal was in a small box. "They were mad as they could get," he recalls. "You could hear their squalling clear across the lot."

Until quarters could be built on campus for the otters, the Goods innocently welcomed the animals into their home, installed them in the basement, and gave them a tub of water in which to play. The otters followed each other, leaping in and out of the tub repeatedly and drying off between dives by rubbing their fur on the carpeted stairs. "The steps were wet for two months," Good told me. They would also sneak into the living room and get beneath the couch, where

they could dry their backs and bellies at the same time. Some who have kept otters complain that they go where they choose and soon learn to bathe in the toilet bowl and dry themselves between the sheets of the nearest bed. As Gavin Maxwell wrote of his otters in *Ring of Bright Water,* "The greater the extent of confusion they can create about them the more contented they feel."

The otters in Good's house took up residence beneath the washing machine until they began ripping out vital wires and had to be banned from that area. In one of his favorite games, the male otter would crawl under the dresser, lie on his back, and push the bottom drawer open. "Then they both would leap into the drawer," said Good, "and pitch out all the contents." When given ice cubes, they played a form of hockey, pushing the cubes with their noses, banking them off the walls, stealing them from each other, and finally watching them

25

melt and vanish before their uncomprehending eyes. The Goods soon learned, as Gavin Maxwell had, that anything an otter can move it will move, anything it can tip over it will empty, and anything it can tear up it will destroy. All small objects become toys. Every space must be investigated. The only respite comes when the otters sleep, which they do about half the time.

At the university the otters were installed in a pen that was partly outdoors, partly indoors, and equipped with a 5,000-gallon tank. "They were absolutely amazing," Good says. "One thing we learned was that they were tool-users." The male learned to push a box to the wall and use it for escapes. Good and his students wondered if the otter might also stack boxes up to escape. They built a series of smaller boxes with sloping sides and the otter pushed one box up on the other to get elevation enough to escape.

"We had a drop door between the outdoor and indoor sections of the pen," Good says, "so we could shut them off when we wanted to clean part of the enclosure. The doors were raised with a rope through a pulley on the ceiling. One day one of the students showed the male otter how to open the door. After that the otter would pull the rope, lift the door, and dash out before the door dropped."

Next, the researchers moved the pulley back toward the middle of the room, putting the pull rope eight feet from the drop door. The otter opened the door but could not reach it in time to get out before it dropped. After a few failures, however, the otter held the rope in his mouth while he ran up to the door and escaped.

"If you keep an otter," says Good, "you can expect to be bitten." One of the Ohio State University graduate students, Robert A. Hall, once reported that several times when he was holding one of Professor Good's otters, it grabbed his cheek or shoulder with its teeth. "I merely growled in a low voice, 'Cut that out,' and it would release me," Hall said. The bite can be severe because otters are equipped with sharp teeth and powerful jaws, for capturing and holding prey and tearing food apart.

Gavin Maxwell tells of putting on three pairs of gloves, including a heavy pair of leather flying gauntlets, the day he decided to take away an eel one of his otters was dragging upstairs: "He bit just once and let go; the canines of his upper and lower jaws passed through the three layers of glove, through the skin, through the muscle and bone, and met in the middle of my hand with an audible crunch." The otter had bro-

ken two bones in Maxwell's hand.

Good once took his female otter to a veterinarian for treatment of an infection. "We decided," he said, "that instead of administering a general anesthetic I should hold her down while he treated her." They quickly learned that it is not possible for a man to immobilize, by sheer physical strength, an otter one-tenth his weight. The squalling otter twisted and turned in her loose skin no matter how she was held. The veterinarian decided to take a turn holding the otter, and he gathered her up by the loose fur of the back, as he was accustomed to do with other animals, whereupon the otter promptly sank her teeth into his slightly protruding belly and hung on. When he tried to pull her away, he only stretched his own middle to the limit. The veterinarian was left with a set of four deep tooth marks.

Any consideration of a wild animal's place in this crowded world is reduced eventually to a discussion of food habits and possible conflicts with people. Wrathful fishermen have persecuted the otter for centuries. During the rule of Edward II in the fourteenth

"Behaviorists may tell us that otters do not really play as we play, that they are responding to instinctive drives and that their frenzied play has survival value, sharpening reflexes, building muscles, fine-tuning the ability to maneuver. But who is to say that otters do not have fun?"

century, English landed gentry kept packs of hounds to kill otters, believing that in this way they were preserving the fish of the rivers. Later, otter hunting became a sport in itself. The English even developed a breed of big, shaggy, web-footed hounds especially for killing otters in the water. Otterhounds, however, were a poor match for an otter on a one-to-one basis. So the hound pack included fox hounds for trailing the otter, poodles for routing them from their burrows, and perhaps half a dozen otterhounds for the kill. A pack of twelve or fifteen dogs all had to work in concert to find and kill otters one at a time. Otter hunting reached its peak in great Britain in the latter half of the nineteenth century, according to *The Complete Dog Book,* the official publication of the American Kennel Club.

Condemnation of otters by Wisconsin trout fishermen once prompted that state's wildlife biologists to study the food habits of the otter. Biologists there, as well as in Michigan and Minnesota, collected from trappers the carcasses of hundreds of otters and analyzed the stomach contents. From these and other studies, investigators determined that the otter is an opportunist and what it eats depends on seasonal abundance. Crayfish are at the top of its list of preferred foods. It also eats frogs and insects. Much of the year fish may indeed provide the bulk of the otter's diet, but the studies show that otters most frequently take not game fish but the more easily captured forage fish and small fish. While otters are known to eat trout, it is a minor factor in their diet, and there is little evidence that they are ever a major factor in reducing trout populations.

Observers studying otters in large tanks conclude that the animals can see only short distances underwater, and that a fish more than a few feet away is safe unless it moves. Motionless, the fish is just another underwater object. Probably, like many mammals, otters have vision that is geared to movement, and they may even be able to recognize different kinds of fish by the way they move through the water. Neither speed nor evasive maneuvering can save a fish from the twisting, turning otter, as the mammal can swim even faster than the fish.

In *The World of the Otter,* Ed Park tells of watching an otter outswim a school of trout in a large pool and outdistance the fish on the straightaway: "The speed of that otter in its last dash was fantastic. I no longer doubt the claim that an otter can outswim a fish." Although no one can be certain what the top speed of an otter might be, it can swim at least as fast as a man can walk, and otter watchers commonly place the speed at six or seven miles an hour. This, of course, is done underwater, where the otter is at its best. There will be no ripple to mark its passing, only a swift, dark form in the water below.

More often, however, the otter cruises at a relaxed pace, swimming alternately on its belly, back, and side, or arching down to inspect some half-hidden crevice or poke about beneath a log or rock. No other land mammal can outswim the river otter.

Biologist Theodore N. Bailey spent days sitting beside the tank on the campus at Ohio State, studying the movements and behavior of the two otters. "In swimming," he reported, "the entire force of propulsion is from the action of the hind feet with a slight 'sculling' action from the tail. The hind feet bend mainly at the ankle joint so there is little movement of the tibia and very little from the femur as the feet move in a vertical plane. The tail is held straight out from the body, and the forelegs are held palms up against the body, thus giving the otter a very streamlined form."

The otter may swim at top speed, then suddenly roll over onto its back and coast upside down, still adroitly steering around obstructions in its path. Or when alone, it may play by rolling into a ball, with head tucked up under the base of the tail, and revolving over and over in the water. Its feet are small, and webbing between the toes gives added push and maneuverability. The otter's strong thick tail is a rudder as well as an aid in propulsion. Swimming otters are exceedingly strong for their size. One captive otter was observed to push a forty-pound concrete block along the floor of its tank by using its front feet. When the block rolled over onto the otter, it easily pushed the weight aside and escaped.

In the wild, otters have a habit of wandering along riverbanks and lakeshores, marking with their scent a mound of earth, a twist of grass, or a convenient rock beside the trail—signposts to be read by other otters, and sometimes by trappers as well.

Otters travel year-round. There is no reason for them to hibernate, because they are winterized. Their coat consists of a dense layer of fine fur beneath a layer of heavier guardhairs, and under the skin they have a layer of fat to give them added protection. In icy weather they can hunt through the coldest days. In northern climates, however, otters seem to vanish from sight as rivers and lakes freeze. They are still active, but now their food supplies are hidden away under the ice and their dens have underwater entrances. On these winter hunting trips underwater, the otters must have air every few minutes, and they utilize pockets of air that are trapped beneath the ice.

Otters are vocal animals; they hiss, purr, whistle, growl, and squall. The squall, according to Good, may indicate anything from dissatisfaction to fury. They have a chirping noise by which they call each other, and a low-pitched humming or muttering that perhaps helps family groups keep together.

The family relationships are close, especially those between mother and pups. At two years of age, females begin having their annual litters, and they may continue to do so for many years. The young, usually two or three and occasionally five, are born in spring in the dark privacy of the burrow. They are already covered with their first fur, but are blind and helpless for five or six weeks. The female keeps her new young warm and safe by curling around them with her body, and if there is danger she also covers them with her head. During this early period the father is expelled from the family group. He comes back some months later to join in the group games and family travels, and helps to teach the young to catch fish and locate other tasty morsels in the mud.

One might think that otters are born swimmers. But the young sometimes must be dragged bodily into the water for the first time—if not kicking and screaming, at least highly reluctant. At first the mother tries trickery. Her pups line up and watch as she disappears into the water, then reappears carrying a crayfish. She drops the delicacy on the bank and lets it roll back into the water. A hungry pup, or one especially bold, may slide into the water and flounder around trying to capture the crayfish. Or it may stay on the bank complaining.

If the female cannot bait a pup into the water this way, she will nudge it toward the water's edge. Failing in these gentle efforts, she will, in desperation, grasp her recalcitrant offspring by the scruff of the neck and drag it protesting into the water. Once in the water, the youngster soon gains confidence and learns that the water holds security, food, and everlasting opportunities for a splashing good time.

Otters can outswim fish. "The entire force of propulsion is from the action of the hind feet with a slight 'sculling' action from the tail . . . the forelegs are held palms up against the body, thus giving the otter a very streamlined form."

29

DON'T MESS WITH MOTHER MOOSE

PHOTOGRAPHY BY DAVID C. FRITTS

At first there were two. The twin moose calves, wobbling on spindly legs to their mother's teats, were born in mid-May in the still-leafless brush bordering the Savage River in Denali National Park. But one calf had soon fallen prey to a grizzly bear, not an unusual occurrence in the Alaska wilderness. In one Denali study area, researchers report that of every one hundred moose calves born in the spring, only ten to fifteen survive to the fall, and half of those that perish will be killed by bears.

Not content with claiming the first calf, this grizzly later returned for its sibling, cornering the cow and her youngster at river's edge. It was the straw that broke the camel's back—or, rather, raised mother moose's hackles. Charging the bear, diverting it from the helpless calf, she lashed out with her front feet, sending the grizzly limping away.

JAVELINA: SOUTHERN

TEXT BY GEORGE LAYCOCK · PHOTOGRAPHY BY STEPHEN J. KRASEMANN

The javelina may win no beauty prize at the county fair, but it leads a far better life than its swill-fed cousin.

The javelina, or collared peccary, looks like the scruffiest little roughneck in the neighborhood, and may be. When grown, this agile pig of cactus patch and scrub oak thickets weighs perhaps fifty pounds and stands twenty inches high at the shoulders.

Millions of years have gone by since the javelina and eastern swine had a common ancestor. The family resemblance is still there, but the javelina lacks the size and conformation to make it a contender at the county fair. It has a compact body, set on spindly legs, a head that is oversized, a neck almost nonexistent, and a stub of a tail scarcely visible.

Javelinas often run in bands of fifteen or twenty. But they do have family squabbles, and from the thickets where they feed come squeals of pain and protest as they shove each other aside or rip their neighbor's hide with straight, sharp teeth.

Left undisturbed, the little band of grunting javelinas roots along, gathering and consuming all edibles within reach. Acorns, mesquite beans, nuts, berries, cactus (spines included), grubs, snakes, toads, and birds' eggs are all high-risk items in its path. The choice of food depends on what the season offers. Prickly pear is a favorite, providing both nourishment and moisture.

The main breeding season comes in February and March, and the pigs, usually twins, arrive in July or August, when food is green from summer rains.

The javelina's range extends from southern Texas, New Mexico, and Arizona into Argentina. It once flourished as far north as Arkansas. Fields and roads broke up its habitat, and uncontrolled hunting reduced the population.

Throughout its range the animal is hunted for its hide, which can be fashioned into quality leather goods, and for the meat which some say is about as tough as its hide. In Texas, New Mexico, and Arizona it is managed as a game animal, and this protection helped it to rebuild its population.

Its cousin, the swine—corn-fed and straw-bedded—is safe from want or fear of coyote and bobcat, but the javelina may lead the better life. There is something to be said for living wild and running free.

ROUGHNECKS

Elk, South Dakota

BEAUTIFUL BONES

PHOTOGRAPHY BY LARRY WEST

"I brought home the bleached bones as my symbols of the desert. To me they are as beautiful as anything I know. To me they are strangely more living than the animals walking around—hair, eyes and all with their tails switching. The bones seem to cut sharply to the center of something that is keenly alive on the desert even tho' it is vast and empty and untouchable—and knows no kindness with all its beauty."

—Georgia O'Keeffe

White-tailed deer, Michigan

Blue jay, Michigan

Raccoon, Michigan

Blacktail prairie dog, South Dakota

Snapping turtle, Michigan

Bison, South Dakota

UNDER THE RUTTING MOON

TEXT BY JOHN MADSON · PHOTOGRAPHY BY ERWIN AND PEGGY BAUER

The shortening days of autumn bring changes to the mule deer. All summer they have ranged through the parks, forests, and high meadows of the Rockies, growing fat and strong again after the hard winter, their bay coats sleek and shining. The fawns of June have been weaned and are no longer wearing the dappled coats of babyhood; their mothers are coming into "the blue," their summer coats replaced by gray winter pelage. Still, life goes on much as it had. Everything is serene.

And then, suddenly, there are bucks.

They seem to materialize overnight into what had been a world of does and fawns. For months the bucks had been timid and retiring, their growing antlers sheathed in vel-

vet. Now those antlers are unsheathed and ready for the wars of November, each mature buck crowned with a rack of sharp-tined, polished bone that is helm, lance, and sword, his badge of authority, his proclamation of maleness to all of his kind. Since spring he has come from meek obscurity to center stage in one prodigious leap through the seasons.

A young buck new at the mating game is diffident but hopeful, lacking in confidence but ready and willing to learn. His antlers reflect his status: Light of beam and modest of tine, they are the training equipment of a squire rather than the heavy weapons of the seasoned knight. The young buck knows this, and approaches a mature buck with

A buck mule deer confronts another buck (opposite page) and marks a shrub (above) with its antlers.

49

Unlike contests between most other male animals, the battles of big mule deer can result in serious injury—or even death should the antlers become locked.

A mule deer buck scents a doe in estrus and will approach her from behind, neck outstretched and head low, uttering a version of a fawn's distress call. The approach is shown on the part-title page—page 9.

reverential awe. Carrying on the analogy of squire and knight, one or the other may suggest a practice joust. This, according to the eminent Canadian biologist Valerius Geist, "has nothing in common with fighting or the settling of dominance rank." It occurs between bucks that are already ranked, usually by a difference in body size, and has no more to do with actual combat than friendly arm wrestling in the corner tavern has with an all-out barroom brawl.

But if another mature buck of the same size and lordly mien as one tending a doe happens to wander into the neighborhood, the battle is joined. There is a clash of arms, each powerful deer straining mightily to assert his will. Unlike contests between most other male animals, the battles of big mule deer can result in serious injury or even death. If their antlers should become inextricably locked under spring tension as a result of the powerful lunges, both bucks are doomed. This is rare, but the slashing and goring of the combatants is not. The freshly tanned hide of one five-year-old buck showed a total of forty-seven new and old

wounds that had at least penetrated his skin.

Unlike elk, mule deer bucks do not form harems. They practice a serial polygyny in which a buck must find a doe, determine if she is in or near estrus, and then actively court her until she can be bred.

During this courtship it is to the buck's advantage to advertise his presence as little as possible and to attract no competition. On the other hand, it's in the doe's interest to play the field, for this will promote intense male competition and help ensure mating with the strongest and most vigorous of the bucks. To do this she must roam more than usual, make more noise than usual, and have a rather conspicuous estrus. Yet, when all this attracts a buck, he tries his best to keep her quiet, secluded, and to himself. He is likely to approach her with great courtesy, head low and eyes averted (it's not polite to stare), making every effort to avoid spooking her, for that could draw the attention of another large buck.

A mature, rutting mule deer buck at close quarters must be an awesome thing to a doe that may weigh only half as much. So how can he assure her that there is no need for alarm? Some biologists think the buck appeals to the mother in her.

All mule deer, even newborn fawns, have distinct facial markings. In the adults these markings are much stronger in bucks than does—and a mature mule deer buck can be said to have a sort of super baby face. As he slowly approaches a doe from the rear, neck outstretched and head low, he may utter a soft, deep version of a fawn's distress call.

The doe, then, is aware of a very large, somewhat baby-faced deer behind her, crooning what might be construed as masculine baby talk. And in spite of those heavy shoulders, thick neck, and regal spread of gleaming antlers, it's hard to avoid the anthropomorphic conclusion that she thinks the big bruiser is cute!

II
BIRDS OF MANY FEATHERS

BLUE JAY: THE "GAY DECEIVER"

TEXT BY LES LINE · PHOTOGRAPHY BY TERRENCE DUFFY

"Who could imagine," John James Audubon wondered of the blue jay, "that a form so graceful, arrayed by nature in a garb so resplendent, should harbor so much mischief; that selfishness, duplicity, and malice should form the moral accompaniments of so much physical perfection! Yet so it is, and how like beings of a much higher order are these gay deceivers." For *The Birds of America,* Audubon painted a trio of blue jays, each "enjoying the fruits of his knavery, sucking the egg which he has pilfered from the nest of some innocent dove or harmless partridge."

And so, for all time, one of our most beautiful birds was branded a rogue and a thief. "He is more tyrannical than brave," Audubon continued, "and like most boasters, domineers over the feeble, dreads the strong, and flies even from his equals. In many cases, in fact, he is a downright coward. The cardinal will challenge him, and beat him off the ground. The robin and mockingbird, and many others, although inferior in strength, never allow him to approach their nest with impunity; and the jay, to be even with them, creeps silently to it in their absence, and devours their eggs and young whenever he finds an opportunity."

There are, however, those who claim the blue jay was libeled. In a comprehensive study published by the U.S. Department of Agriculture in 1897, F.E.L. Beal examined the stomach contents of 292 blue jays collected in every month of the year from twenty-two states and Canada. The jays' food, he reported, was composed of exactly one-third animal matter and two-thirds vegetable matter. "The animal food is chiefly made up of insects, with a few spiders, myr-iopods, snails, and small vertebrates, such as fish, salamanders, tree frogs, mice, and birds. . . . Everything was carefully examined which might by any possibility indicate that birds or eggs had been eaten, but remains of birds were found in only two, and the shells of small birds' eggs in three of the 292 stomachs. . . . The most striking point in the study of the food of the blue jay is the discrepancy between the testimony of field observers concerning the bird's nest-robbing proclivities and the results of stomach examinations."

Unquestionably, the truth lies closer to Professor Beal's careful analyses, which were intended to assess the economic impact of common birds on agriculture, than to Audubon's vivid prose. Blue jays eat great quantities of beetles, grasshoppers, and caterpillars, of nuts, berries, and grain. And, as this extraordinary picture proves, they will on occasion rob nests. Terry Duffy was photographing the activities at a Baltimore oriole nest in Ohio, where the adults were arriving every few minutes to feed their nestlings. Both parents were absent when a jay landed on the edge of the nest and, in the space of three or four seconds, grabbed a nestling and flew off. When the blue jay reappeared a few minutes later, it was driven off by the orioles. But when Duffy checked the next day, a second oriole nestling was missing and the nest was abandoned.

This photograph, to some, will be the final evidence necessary to convict Audubon's "gay deceiver" as the Attila of songbirds. I, for one, forgive the blue jay its trespasses, for without its flashing color, its raucous screams and sweet warbles, its unpredictable behavior, my woodlands would be impoverished.

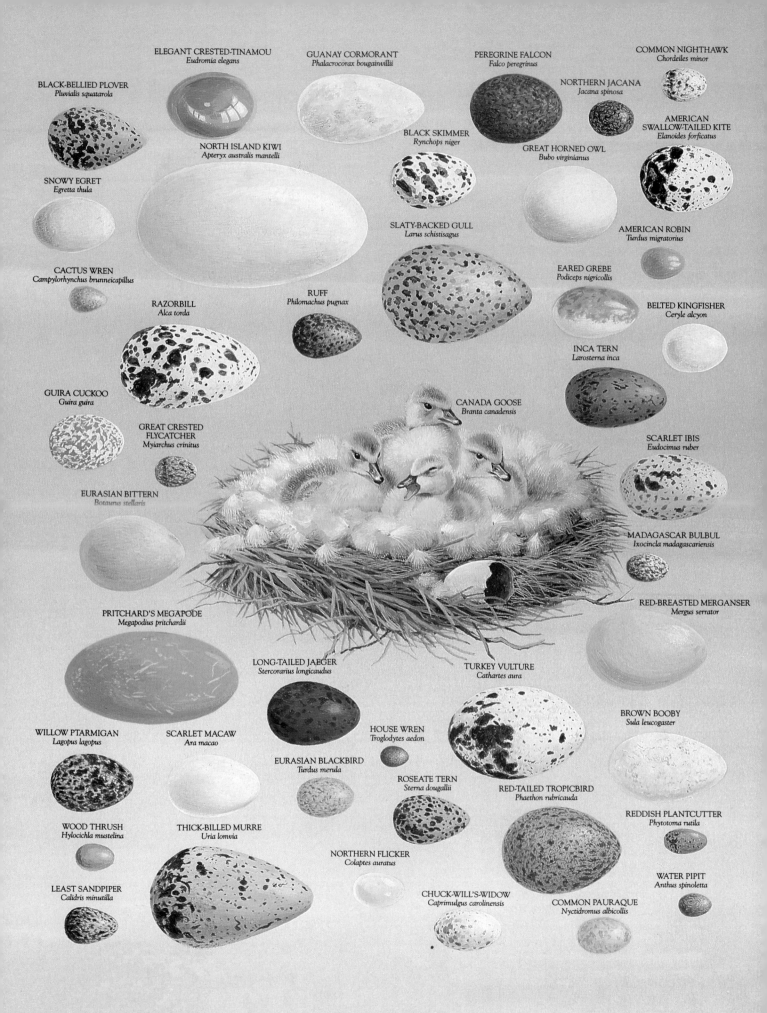

BLACK-BELLIED PLOVER
Pluvialis squatarola

ELEGANT CRESTED-TINAMOU
Eudromia elegans

GUANAY CORMORANT
Phalacrocorax bougainvillii

PEREGRINE FALCON
Falco peregrinus

COMMON NIGHTHAWK
Chordeiles minor

NORTHERN JACANA
Jacana spinosa

NORTH ISLAND KIWI
Apteryx australis mantelli

BLACK SKIMMER
Rynchops niger

GREAT HORNED OWL
Bubo virginianus

AMERICAN
SWALLOW-TAILED KITE
Elanoides forficatus

SNOWY EGRET
Egretta thula

SLATY-BACKED GULL
Larus schistisagus

AMERICAN ROBIN
Turdus migratorius

CACTUS WREN
Campylorhynchus brunneicapillus

RUFF
Philomachus pugnax

EARED GREBE
Podiceps nigricollis

BELTED KINGFISHER
Ceryle alcyon

RAZORBILL
Alca torda

INCA TERN
Larosterna inca

CANADA GOOSE
Branta canadensis

GUIRA CUCKOO
Guira guira

SCARLET IBIS
Eudocimus ruber

GREAT CRESTED
FLYCATCHER
Myiarchus crinitus

EURASIAN BITTERN
Botaurus stellaris

MADAGASCAR BULBUL
Ixocincla madagascariensis

RED-BREASTED MERGANSER
Mergus serrator

PRITCHARD'S MEGAPODE
Megapodius pritchardii

LONG-TAILED JAEGER
Stercorarius longicaudus

TURKEY VULTURE
Cathartes aura

BROWN BOOBY
Sula leucogaster

WILLOW PTARMIGAN
Lagopus lagopus

SCARLET MACAW
Ara macao

HOUSE WREN
Troglodytes aedon

EURASIAN BLACKBIRD
Turdus merula

ROSEATE TERN
Sterna dougallii

RED-TAILED TROPICBIRD
Phaethon rubricauda

REDDISH PLANTCUTTER
Phytotoma rutila

WOOD THRUSH
Hylocichla mustelina

THICK-BILLED MURRE
Uria lomvia

NORTHERN FLICKER
Colaptes auratus

WATER PIPIT
Anthus spinoletta

LEAST SANDPIPER
Calidris minutilla

CHUCK-WILL'S-WIDOW
Caprimulgus carolinensis

COMMON PAURAQUE
Nyctidromus albicollis

WHY IS A ROBIN'S EGG BLUE?

TEXT BY BERND HEINRICH · PAINTINGS BY ARTHUR SINGER

The four tiny eggs that were cradled on feathers in a nest of moss, lichens, and spider webs were decorated more beautifully than any I had ever seen before. They were greenish-blue, marked with purple and lavender blotches and black scratchy squiggles. A cascading chaffinch song rang from the surrounding beech forest on that beautiful spring morning and heightened the sensations I felt when I discovered the eggs.

I was then eight years old, and in the following years I became obsessed with collecting the nests and eggs of other species. The more I found, the greater the obsession became. Each find rewarded me with revelations about the species' intricacies and its individualities.

Later, while in grammar school and high school in central Maine, I continued to collect songbird nests and eggs. I did not dare let the authorities at my boarding school know, in part perhaps because my pleasure was so great that it did not seem it could be morally right. I spent endless days in the woods watching birds and hunting for nests. I kept my carefully tended illicit collection hidden under the floorboards of an abandoned shed. (At that time I did not know anything about wildlife laws.) Now, thirty-five years later, this collection of ninety-six species of Maine land bird eggs with their nests is still in excellent condition, in the museum and teaching collections of the University of Vermont. Although I long ago stopped collecting wild bird eggs, my fascination and enthusiasm have not been erased. I still collect these jewels, but only on film. The main excitement now is in trying to find a coherent system of filing it all in the mind. And as I am a biologist, the filing system I use is based on evolution.

First one sees the diversity. The four eggs of the scarlet tanager, in a cup of loose twigs lined with dark rootlets, are sky blue and spotted with light brown in a ring at the larger end. The four eggs of the eastern pee-wee are a light cream, with a wreath of reddish-brown and lavender spots about the larger end. These colors are set against a perfectly round nest-cup decorated with gray-green lichens. Woodpecker and kingfisher eggs, from holes excavated in trees and sandbanks, respectively, are translucent white without any trace of markings. The different colors, or lack of them, are products of evolution. What were the selective pressures that produced them?

Although the eggs of many species of songbirds have characteristic colors that are fairly uniform within a clutch, I noticed that those of most hawks differed radically within the same nest, even as much as they differed between species. One egg of a broad-winged hawk, for example, had distinct dark brown or purple splotches. Another in the same clutch had chocolate brown spots and squiggles. A third had purple or brown washes, and still another might be almost colorless. The same variety of colors—but in greens, blues, grays, and browns—was present in any one clutch of common raven's and common crow's eggs.

These combinations of markings and colors on bird eggs seemed like creativity gone berserk. Why should the color of an eggshell matter to a bird? Why, indeed, have any color at all? There must have been reasons to add the color, or else specialized glands to apply color would not have evolved. So why are robins' eggs pale blue, flickers' eggs pure white, and loons' eggs dark olive green?

Birds' eggs are marked by pigments secreted from the walls of the oviduct. The egg remains uncolored until just before being laid, when it traverses the region of the uterus. The pressure of the egg squeezes the pigment out of the uterine glands onto the eggshell, and the motion of the egg affects the color patterns. It is as if innumerable brushes hold still while the canvas moves. If the egg remains still there are spots, and if it moves while the glands continue secreting, then lines and scrawls result.

Egg color is under genetic control, and there is considerable genetic plasticity. Strains of domestic chickens have been devel-

"Why should the color of an eggshell matter to a bird? Why, indeed, have any color at all? There must have been reasons to add the color, or else specialized glands to apply color would not have evolved." (Paintings of bird eggs and European cuckoo from "Birds of the World," © 1961 Western Publishing Company Inc. Used by permission. Original art courtesy Lucille Ogle.)

oped that lay eggs tinted blue, green, and olive, as well as the more familiar white and brown.

It is not surprising that Charles Darwin, with his wide-ranging interests, also thought about the adaptive significance of the coloration of birds' eggs. Since coloration is generally absent in hole-nesters such as woodpeckers, parrots, kingfishers, barbets, and honey guides, he supposed that the pigmentation on the eggs of open-nesters acts as a sunscreen to protect the embryo. The British ornithologist David Lack, in turn, believed the white coloration of eggs of hole-nesters allowed the birds to see their eggs in the dark. Even if it is advantageous for birds to see their eggs in the dark (which I doubt), we are still left to explain the tremendous differences in colors and patterns found, especially in the species that do not nest in holes. Why isn't one sunscreen best? And if so, why don't all use it? And why are some hole-nesters' eggs spotted? Perhaps, as Austin L. Rand, former chief curator of zoology at the Field Museum in Chicago, has said: "Like some of the specific differences in nest-building, variations in egg color are simply expressions of the general tendency of birds toward diversity." This idea, too, might be right, but if so it is only a small part of the proverbial elephant that the six blind men try to describe by touch. With regard to egg coloring, we are still blind, and we all touch the elephant in different places.

One summer when I was motoring across the country with my family, we stopped in Yellowstone National Park. My most vivid memory was of walking across a sedge meadow bordered by stunted black spruce. I was captivated by the sound of a sandhill crane trumpeting, and the song of the Wilson's snipe high in the air. Looking down, I saw a nest in the mossy sedge. It contained four olive green eggs generously marked with blackish-brown. It was the nest of the Wilson's snipe, and the eggs blended beautifully with the dark green vegetation of this boggy meadow. Later on, we camped in numerous gravel pits and along roadside turnoffs by streambeds and sandy parking lots—habitat where killdeers nest. A killdeer perched on the ground over its eggs is not difficult to spot. But the adult slips off the nest when anyone comes near, and the bare eggs are something else. Colored a drab buff and profusely spotted with black, the four eggs are not easy to make out in a depression filled with pebbles.

Experiments confirm that the color of some birds' eggs conceals them from predators. In a famous experiment, Niko Tinbergen distributed equal numbers of naturally spotted eggs of black-headed gulls, uniformly khaki-colored eggs, and white eggs near a gull colony and then recorded the predation by carrion crows and herring gulls on these unguarded eggs. The natural eggs suffered the least predation.

We might reasonably assume that the color of snipe, killdeer, and gull eggs is adaptive for camouflage, and that it evolved under selective pressure from visually oriented egg predators. But why then do other ground-nesting birds—most ducks and many grouse—have unmarked eggs that cannot be considered camouflaged by any stretch of the imagination? Perhaps part of the answer is that most of these birds hide their nests in dense vegetation, and the incubating female's own body is a camouflage blanket.

So far so good. But there is a hitch. Ducks and grouselike birds usually lay more than a dozen eggs per clutch. If the female started to sit on the eggs as soon as the first ones were laid, in order to hide them, the chicks would then hatch out over a period of up to two weeks. It is necessary for the eggs to hatch synchronously, and to accomplish this, the hen must not sit on the eggs until the last one is laid. So how are the eggs protected from predators? A pet mallard hen gave me a hint. She built a nest by scraping leaves together under a bush by the front window. Being well fed, she layed enormous clutches of creamy pale green eggs. But I never saw the eggs directly. Each morning before she left, after laying an egg, she used her bill to pull leaves from around the nest to cover the eggs completely. The leaves were better camouflage than spots on the eggs or her own body could ever be. I do not know if all ducks and grouse cover their eggs in a similar manner, but their nests are usually mere depressions, with loose vegetation that could serve as a cover. Not all grouse have uncamouflaged eggs, though. Those of the willow and rock ptarmigans, for example, are heavily blotched and marbled with blackish-brown. (I've been told that ptarmigans leave their eggs uncovered before they incubate.)

Many birds with nests that have no loose material with which to cover the eggs also have unmarked, uncamouflaged eggs. They include hummingbirds, pigeons, and doves. But these birds only lay two eggs per clutch, and they incubate as soon as the first egg is laid. Perhaps because none of their eggs are normally left uncovered, there has been no need to color them for camouflage.

The best explanation for the lack of color

and markings on hole-nesters' eggs and those of birds that lay small clutches is probably simply that there was no need for color, so none evolved. Yet, as already mentioned, some birds that nest in holes lay spotted eggs. All of these birds, however, build nests inside the holes. (True hole-nesters excavate their own holes and lay white eggs without adding any nest material.) I suspect, therefore, that the spots are evolutionary baggage. They tell us that these birds had previously been open-nesters who switched to hole-nesting. But they retained the habit of building nests, as well as the coloration of their eggs, because there was no great selective pressure for change.

While coloring and markings are primarily for camouflage, they can also function to make something stand out like a red flag. Along the coast of Maine the harbors and inlets are dotted with the floats of thousands of lobster traps. There are green floats, red floats, white floats, striped red-white floats, and so on. The large numbers of traps and the featureless environment of the open water make it impractical for a lobsterman to find his traps by remembering their precise locations. Each fisherman uses a different color pattern for his floats so he can quickly home in on his own traps.

On our Atlantic and Pacific coasts, on ad-

jacent islands, and in Europe, there are murres that nest on the ledges and sea cliffs in colonies of hundreds of thousands. Several species of colonial cliff-nesting murres (as well as the extinct great auk) have eggs that vary endlessly in colors and markings. The ground color of the eggs varies from creamy to white, reddish, warm ocher, pale bluish, or even deep greenish-blue. The markings upon this ground color, in turn, may be blotches, spots, or intricate interlacing lines of yellowish-brown, bright red, dark brown, or black. Some eggs are totally unmarked. (When a murre loses the one egg—its entire clutch—it lays another, and this one is colored like the first.) In contrast, the eggs of the closely related auklets of various species, which nest in burrows or rock crevices, have few or no markings.

Chester A. Reed, one of the early oologists during the heyday of egg collecting in the last century, says of the murres: "The eggs are laid as closely as possible on the ledges where the incubating birds sit upright, in long rows like an army on guard. As long as each bird succeeds in finding an egg to cover on its return home, it is doubtful if the bird either knows, or cares, whether it is its own or not." Thanks to experiments some twenty-five years ago by Beat Tschantz of the Zoological Institute of the University of Bern, Switzerland, we know that Reed was wrong.

Eggs of a broad-winged hawk. The eggs of most hawks differ radically within the same nest, even as much as they differ between species.

ior of some birds—herring gulls, for example—which accept almost anything of any color even remotely resembling an egg.

Recognition of eggs by their color pattern has evolved in some other birds under an entirely different set of selective pressures: The need to detect and destroy the eggs of parasites.

Reproductive success in murres is enhanced if the females can pick out their own uniquely colored eggs. In contrast, under the selective pressure of brood parasitism, a bird's reproductive success is enhanced if it can recognize the eggs of other birds in its clutch and discard them. The possibility of parasitism would place selective pressure on the host bird to detect the odd-colored eggs. This would, in turn, put pressure on the parasite to produce eggs resembling those of its host.

The European cuckoo and its hosts may have evolved the most sophisticated egg-color matching. The European cuckoo never builds a nest of its own. Among the various birds it victimizes are wagtails, which have white eggs densely spotted in gray; bramblings, whose pale blue eggs have heavy reddish spots; and European redstarts, with blue unspotted eggs. The cuckoo eggs found in these nests usually match closely those of their hosts. The accuracy of the imitations is sometimes so good that even the human eye has difficulty in distinguishing the eggs of the parasite from those of the host.

It was long a mystery how such color matching could occur, for surely cuckoos do not paint their eggs to match those of their intended victims. The real answer, however, is almost as bizarre: In any given area the cuckoos are made up of reproductively isolated subgroups called "gentes," whose females restrict their parasitism to particular hosts. It is believed that the gentes arose through geographic isolation, although at the present time two or more gentes may occupy the same area. A given female always lays the same-colored eggs, and almost always with the same host species.

In European passerine birds heavily parasitized by cuckoos, there has been potent selective pressure to foil the parasitism. Hosts have developed a strong attention to egg-color code, abandoning many nests with cuckoo eggs or throwing the cuckoo eggs out. This puts stronger pressure on the cuckoos to produce even better egg mimicry. Only the well-matched eggs are accepted.

Parasitism in North America is no less severe, but the principal parasite of songbirds, the brown-headed cowbird, thus far has not evolved egg-color mimicry. Never-

A parasitic European cuckoo removes an egg from its host's nest, and a lesser whitethroat feeds a cuckoo fledgling. "The European cuckoo and its hosts have evolved the most sophisticated egg-color matching."

The murres no more incubate each other's eggs than the lobstermen tend each other's traps. Both use color and markings to identify their property. Tschantz switched eggs and found that if an egg of a different color or marking pattern was substituted for the bird's own egg, that egg was rejected, but another egg with a similar pattern was accepted. But the birds don't have innate recognition of their own eggs. For example, if a murre's egg is marked with white feces in small increments, the bird learns the new color pattern and will reject eggs of its own original pattern. This fine discrimination by murres stands in strong contrast to the behav-

A brown-headed cowbird's egg in a hermit thrush's nest. "It would be easier to recognize a stranger's egg if all the eggs within a clutch were similar."

theless, the cowbird is a highly successful parasite. It is one of the most common of our native passerine birds, and it is also one of the most widely distributed. According to Herbert Friedmann, a long-time student of avian brood parasitism, it parasitizes more than 350 species and subspecies of birds. Some species suffer heavily. Up to 78 percent of all song sparrow nests in some areas have been victimized by this parasite. The cowbird, however, also lays eggs occasionally in the nests of such unlikely potential hosts as the spotted sandpiper and ruby-crowned kinglet, as well as in many other nests where its eggs regularly get damaged or evicted. In short, it wastes many eggs. The cowbird is partial to open habitat, having spread east from the short-grass prairies in the Midwest only in the last two or three centuries.

At this point in the evolutionary race, only some of the potential victims of the brown-headed cowbird have evolved appropriate egg-rejection responses. Stephen I. Rothstein of the University of California at Santa Barbara determined this by making plaster of Paris eggs and painting them to mimic cowbird eggs. He deposited these in a total of 640 nests of forty-three species. He found that two-thirds of the passerine birds accepted the parasite eggs, while only one-

61

Although catbirds reject cowbird eggs placed with their own, in one study a catbird accepted a full clutch of cowbird eggs. Then a catbird egg added to the nest was rejected.

fourth consistently rejected them. Some birds, like the red-winged blackbird, yellow warbler, phoebe, and barn swallow, consistently accepted both fake and real parasite eggs, while others, like the catbird, robin, and kingbird, consistently rejected them. Since the birds were either consistent "acceptors" or "rejectors," he speculated that once the rejection behavior was genetically coded, it was of such great advantage that it spread rapidly and became fixed.

Early on in the relationship between parasite and potential host, a lack of color matching of the eggs is probably not necessary to ensure the parasite's success. However, eventually, as with the European cuckoo, similarity becomes important. It is doubtful if rejection can occur if—initially by chance and ultimately by evolution—the parasite and host eggs are exactly alike. Indeed, song sparrows and brown-headed cowbirds have eggs that are similar in size and dense brown spotting; and this sparrow rarely rejects the cowbird eggs. Both robins and catbirds, which have immaculate blue eggs, on the other hand, almost always do. In contrast, the phoebe, which lays pure white eggs, readily accepts cowbird eggs. But does a phoebe, nesting under a ledge or on a beam under a barn, ever notice the color of its eggs at all?

Since a key component of defense against parasitism involves egg recognition, one would predict that means of detecting foreign eggs would evolve. For example, it would be easier to recognize a stranger's egg if all the eggs within a clutch were similar. Does this help explain the fact that songbirds subject to parasitism have uniform egg coloring, while birds such as hawks, ravens, and crows have a variety of egg colorations in one clutch?

Some sixty years ago Bernhard Rensch, studying mimicry of cuckoo eggs in Germany, wondered whether songbirds could recognize their own eggs. In one experiment he replaced the first three eggs in a nest of the garden warbler with lesser whitethroat eggs. The warbler then ejected its own fourth egg! Rensch concluded that egg rejection was not on the basis of true recognition of a bird's own eggs, but on the basis of the discordance in appearance relative to the other eggs in the nest. But recent experiments by Rothstein show that there is more to the story. Like the murres studied by Tschantz, some songbirds also *learn* the appearance of their own eggs, becoming imprinted on the first egg they see in their nest. In an experiment that showed this most clearly, Rothstein re-

moved all eggs in a catbird nest each day as they were laid, replacing them with cowbird eggs. Although catbirds normally reject cowbird eggs placed in with their own, this catbird accepted a whole clutch of cowbird eggs. Then a single catbird egg added to the cowbird eggs was rejected.

Why don't more birds practice the art of parasitism? As with many historical questions, we don't have an ironclad answer, but we may identify some of the selective processes at work. One possibility is that after a parasite has become established, and through millions of years improved its strategy, the hosts will have such good methods of egg detection that another bird just starting out would have no success. For example, I doubt that the brown-headed cowbird could become established in Europe, because the European birds, under the selective pressure of the cuckoo, have already evolved such a sophisticated egg-recognition system that they would not be fooled by the crude tactics of the cowbird.

There are other implications. For example, a parasite would have a great advantage if it could utilize a variety of hosts. And multiple parasitism would be easy if all the parasite's victims had similar eggs. Any bird lucky enough to have distinctively marked eggs should most easily spot and reject a parasite's eggs. In other words, to avoid parasitism a bird should have eggs that are different from those whose nests the parasite already uses. This would make for variety among different species but uniformity within clutches. And in general these are the patterns we see in nature.

Perhaps there is, after all, an evolutionary reason for the "general tendency of birds toward diversity." Perhaps catbirds' eggs, by being blue, are less camouflaged, but they gain instead by providing a sharp contrast, and so cowbirds' eggs can be detected and evicted.

It will likely not be possible ever to say with any degree of precision why a robin's egg is blue or a kingbird's egg is white and splotched with dark brown and purple. However, the diversity of patterns shows that there are different selective pressures at work. The coloration of birds' eggs reflects a long interplay of forces, in the face of randomness and chance, to produce organization in many parallel evolutionary paths that we now see in different stages. This, in turn, "colors" the mind as well as the eye, and gives eggs an additional beauty that no person's brush could ever impart.

ATLANTIC PUFFIN
Fratercula arctica

KING PENGUIN
Aptenodytes patagonicus

NORTHERN MOCKINGBIRD
Mimus polyglottos

CRESTED CARACARA
Polyborus plancus

WHITE WAGTAIL
Motacilla alba

WHITE-TAILED EAGLE
Haliaeetus albicilla

COMMON GRACKLE
Quiscalus quiscula

BRUSHLAND TINAMOU
Nothoprocta cinerascens

GREAT-TAILED GRACKLE
Quiscalus mexicanus

GREAT TINAMOU
Tinamus major

SCISSOR-TAILED
FLYCATCHER
Tyrannus forficatus

BRITISH STORM-PETREL
Hydrobates pelagicus

COMMON RAVEN
Corvus corax

MACGREGOR'S
BIRD OF PARADISE
Macgregoria pulchra

ARCTIC LOON
Gavia arctica

EURASIAN SKYLARK
Alauda arvensis

GOLDEN EAGLE
Aquila chrysaetos

BLUE-GRAY GNATCATCHER
Polioptila caerulea

AMERICAN WOODCOCK
Scolopax minor

AMERICAN CROW
Corvus brachyrhynchos

YELLOW-BILLED CUCKOO
Coccyzus americanus

ANHINGA
Anhinga anhinga

LIMPKIN
Aramus guarauna

SANDHILL CRANE
Grus canadensis

SMALL-BILLED TINAMOU
Crypturellus parvirostris

EASTERN BLUEBIRD
Sialia sialis

SAGE GROUSE
Centrocercus urophasianus

BROWN PELICAN
Pelecanus occidentalis

HOOPOE
Upupa epops

EUROPEAN BEE-EATER
Merops apiaster

BARN SWALLOW
Hirundo rustica

SPRUCE GROUSE
Dendragapus canadensis

MALLARD
Anas platyrhynchos

DWARF CASSOWARY
Casuarius bennetti

SHARP-TAILED GROUSE
Tympanuchus phasianellus

RED-BREASTED PITTA
Pitta erythrogaster

WHITE-WINGED
TRILLER
Lalage sueurii

GENTOO PENGUIN
Pygoscelis papua

BROAD-BILLED
HUMMINGBIRD
Cynanthus latirostris

OLIVE-SIDED
FLYCATCHER
Contopus borealis

GREAT ANTSHRIKE
Taraba major

RATTLING CISTICOLA
Cisticola chiniana

BLACKBIRDS ARE BEAUTIFUL

PHOTOGRAPHY BY TIM FITZHARRIS

Farmers whose croplands are invaded by hordes of blackbirds undoubtedly would disagree with that statement. Even John James Audubon, in his account of the "red-shouldered marsh blackbird," called it "a bird of the most nefarious propensities." But habitués of the spring marshlands have been moved to wax eloquent over the courtship displays of the male redwing and Audubon's "saffron-headed marsh blackbird." Of the latter, Arthur Cleveland Bent wrote, in his monumental "Life Histories":

"Grasping a tall, upright cane, or perhaps two, in a straddling attitude, he displayed his fine plumage by spreading his black tail and half opening his wings to show the white patches; he leaned forward, pointing his bright yellow head downward until it was almost parallel with his tail and poured out his grotesque love notes. The female seemed indifferent."

And Bent quoted one Charles W. Townsend as writing: "The courtship of the red-winged blackbird centers as distinctly about the display of the scarlet epaulettes as does the courtship of the peacock about the display of his train.... When his love passions are excited he spreads his tail, slightly opens his wings, puffs out all his feathers, and sings his *quonk-quer-ee,* or his still more watery and gurgling song, appropriate to an oozing bog, *ōgle-ŏggle-yer."*

The red-shouldered marsh blackbird is shown at left, the saffron-headed marsh blackbird, below.

65

FOOD FOR FLIGHT

TEXT BY JOHN O. BIDERMAN · PHOTOGRAPHY BY DAVID C. TWICHELL

The sky is a uniform gray, and a fine mist is blowing in our faces when we arrive at the shore. The advancing army has already begun its invasion, establishing its beachhead.

No, this is not the Falklands or Iwo Jima. It is not even anyplace one normally considers exotic. We are in New Jersey; to my snobbish Northeasterner's mind, since this is neither New England nor Florida, we are approximately nowhere, and not much interesting should be going on. Nevertheless, Brian Harrington, a seasoned ornithologist from the Manomet Bird Observatory (on what I consider the more acceptable shore of Cape Cod Bay, just south of Plymouth, Massachusetts), has lured me here by promising a natural-history spectacle he is sure I will find overwhelming. He described it to me prior to the visit, and I think I'm ready for the sights this weekend will bring.

I'm not.

The advancing army here on the Delaware Bay shore of the Cape May peninsula in extreme southern New Jersey is not engaged in combat. To be perfectly blunt, it is more akin to an orgy. Horseshoe crabs by the thousands are engaged in their reproductive bout for the year, coming ashore to burrow in the sand and lay their eggs.

"We've learned something today," Harrington says, looking at the hostile sky, then down at the water. "They must take their cue from the movement of the tides, obviously not from the intensity of light." It is the crabs' second invasion of the day, coinciding with the second incoming tide. They form a swath from along the shore above the water mark to some ten or twelve feet out, a partially submerged road paved with armored arthropods. "Well, what do you think?" I'm too overwhelmed by the sight to respond sensibly; as I was to learn throughout the weekend, one often is reduced to saying, "Wow."

But the horseshoe crabs aren't half the picture. The females, each with a male clasped firmly behind, are together laying uncountable trillions of eggs. It is a gross biological playing of the odds, for only a fraction of the eggs stay buried. The excess is suspended in the water and is washing ashore with seaweed and other detritus. And *that* is the cause of the frenzied, cacophonous scene unfolding on the beach.

Most conspicuous are the laughing gulls, flashy with slate-gray heads, red bills, and loud, raucous calls. There are about 5,000 of them, floating or standing at the water's edge, and they are, in the vernacular, "chowing down." According to folk wisdom, there is not supposed to be any such thing as a free lunch, but for the birds this bounty of eggs seems to be just that.

As we peer down the quarter-mile stretch of sand, the beach appears mottled with undulating gray matter. Harrington has set up a spotting scope on a tripod and trained it down the shore. "Feast your eyes," he says, stepping away so I can look through the eyepiece. I see a carpet of shorebirds—red knots and ruddy turnstones, roughly in a ratio of three to two. They too are feasting on the eggs deposited farther up on the beach by the previous high tide. The birds are pecking rapidly at the sand, gobbling eggs, stopping only long enough to peck at a neighbor that has moved too close.

This event is an annual spectacle, Harrington explained to me, around the time of the new moon or full moon—whichever extreme phase it happens to be—in middle to late May. The invasion of crabs is cued by the high tides pulled by the moon. Gulls that nest in nearby marshes come as opportunists to gorge themselves on the excess eggs. The

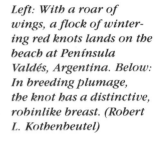

Left: With a roar of wings, a flock of wintering red knots lands on the beach at Península Valdés, Argentina. Below: In breeding plumage, the knot has a distinctive, robinlike breast. (Robert L. Kothenbeutel)

"The advancing army is not engaged in combat. To be perfectly blunt, it is more akin to an orgy. Horseshoe crabs by the thousands are engaged in their reproductive bout for the year, coming ashore to burrow and lay eggs."

shorebirds, meanwhile, are on their way to the high Arctic to nest. This is their main, and final, gathering place on the long journey north, which for some of them began as far south as Tierra del Fuego. At the peak of this gathering, some 200,000 shorebirds may occupy a fifteen-mile stretch of shore, and 60,000 of them may be red knots.

"Let's try to sneak up on that dense group," Harrington says. "See if we can see some bands." Bands are what this trip is about. For nearly a decade, the Manomet ornithologists have been on the trail of the red knot, piecing together the story of its remarkable migration, an annual circuit from the Arctic to lower South America and back. At various stopover places along the way, the researchers have trapped some birds and put bands on their legs, some of them colored or with little adhesive color flags attached. By looking over the feeding flocks with a telescope and finding banded legs, Harrington and his colleague Linda Leddy are finding out what birds have come in and from where. It is work that demands patience in the extreme. "We've been here six days and checked around thirty thousand legs." And how many had bands? "Around two hundred and fifty. We've seen them from every place we've banded—Massachusetts, Florida, Argentina. We should be able to get some good data out of this."

So we are moving closer to the dense flock of knots and turnstones to look at more legs. But the birds are skittish and begin lifting off. There are on this beach some 20,000 shorebirds, and this group we've scared up numbers around 3,000. The sight is awesome, and before I have a chance to catch myself, that word escapes my lips: "Wow"—a helpless utterance common to newcomers viewing this scene. Yet, I was glad to find, after years of springtime visits here, Harrington and Leddy are as unscientifically awed as I am.

We grope for metaphors for the cloud of knots swirling in front of and over us. "A dust storm of monstrous particles," I suggest, admittedly stretching. "A swarm of gnats—or tsetse flies." Harrington simplifies things: "I prefer to think of it as a cloud of knots. To me there really isn't a comparable sight."

Indeed, the poetry of shorebirds and their migration is not a minor part of the Manomet researchers' interest in them. Both Harrington and Leddy reveal the sense of marvel and enthusiasm about their research subjects that imbues most natural historians. "There really isn't a more spectacular long-distance migrant than the red knot," Harrington told me before our trip. "The current migration titleholder is the Arctic tern, which goes from the Arctic to the Antarctic. But it feeds all along the way, and it takes months to complete its journey, all of it at sea level. By contrast, we're certain that most of the American population of knots travels these same distances, sometimes completing four-thousand-mile legs in sixty hours. And we know from studies with radar that they go up to twenty thousand feet to do it. That's one reason for studying them—they're spectacular migrants."

Aside from that, he said, the majority of red knots use just a few stopover areas during their journey, Cape May in the spring being one of them. They congregate by the thousands at those sites. "That means that an environmental disturbance at one stopover place could have a drastic effect on a substantial portion of the population, which right now we estimate at around two hundred thousand birds." (That figure refers to the North American race; the Old World knot is more numerous and widespread.)

These migration gathering sites, which biologists refer to as staging areas, generally are rich in a particular food. Cape May's, of course, is the ephemeral inundation of horseshoe crab eggs. It is food the birds must consume to complete their journeys. Indeed, the knot migration is a story of moving with the changing seasons from one area rich in food to another—the presumed reason for any animal migration, but one that is hard to demonstrate for most birds. Working with shorebirds, the Manomet team has found, is convenient because they are conspicuous, and the scientists can watch and measure what the birds are feeding on.

But figuring out exactly where they stop requires, at least initially, surveying an enormous area. Faced with this, the Manomet researchers organized a volunteer network of birdwatching hobbyists and professional ornithologists, which they named the International Shorebird Survey. The network now has 300 cooperators in twenty nations and commonwealths in the Americas, an organization the Manomet team is proud of.

In addition, they have carried out their own fieldwork over an area as large as the knots occupy. Harrington and his colleagues, often with volunteer help, have worked their home turf of Massachusetts, and they've ventured to New Jersey, Florida, Venezuela, Surinam, and Argentina. Colleagues in the Canadian Wildlife Service study the birds in northern Ontario as well.

The major effort on most of these trips is to get the birds in the hand—worth twice, folk wisdom again tells us, what they are in the field—for purposes of weighing, measuring, feather studying, and, above all, banding. Trapping knots is made somewhat easier by their tendency to stay in close-knit flocks. If you have the right equipment, you can get a lot of them at once. The Manomet team does: They've adapted for the task a rocket net, a device used mostly on large waterfowl and group-nesting birds. It consists of a 60-by-40-foot net, the front end of which is propelled over a flock of resting birds by five rockets, each weighing about six pounds. Of course, the rockets create a boom, and the birds take to the air, but the leading edge of the net usually floats down in front of most of the flock, and the birds are pinned harmlessly to the ground until retrieved by a biologist. On a good shot, Harrington says, they'll get 200 to 300 birds; it takes about five hours to process and release them.

The globe-trotting fieldwork has produced some impressive results. A knot trapped in Massachusetts on its way south on August 7, 1980, was caught again the following April at Península Valdés, in southern Argentina. It evidently returned north to breed again, for the rocket-netters trapped it once more in Massachusetts on July 30, 1981—their first double recovery. "The bird," Harrington remarked, "made banding history." Other sightings attest to the birds' lengthy and swift migrations: Several knots color-banded by Manomet workers at Lagoa do Peixe in southernmost Brazil in early May 1984, were seen at Cape May a mere 15 days later. "It is an eerie feeling," said David Twichell, a Manomet researcher, "to realize that the same birds you're looking at are ones you handled a couple of weeks earlier, fifty-six hundred miles to the south."

Harrington, Leddy, and I have walked through a marsh to the beach and are hiding ourselves like spies in a small clump of reeds, where we've set up telescopes to look at more knot legs. The birds are eating eggs some fifty feet from us.

It is quiet work, peering intently through the scopes at a parade of little metatarsals. The only noise, in fact, is the murmuring from the birds on the shore. Minutes of quiet looking go by. "I need a band fix," Harrington says. It's his term for the virtual euphoria of seeing a banded bird, the only relief for his impatient twitching. "One band sighting can last me a few hours, and if it's a really good one, say an Argentina bird, it makes my day." For the time being he is out of luck. He writes down the ratios of birds banded to birds checked: zero out of thirty, zero out of seventy, zero out of a hundred. Knots and sandpipers keep arriving in groups of fifty or sixty, replenishing the supply of research material for the ornithologists.

The spring orgy of horseshoe crabs on the Cape May beach provides crucial fuel—trillions of "wasted" eggs—for the final leg of the red knot's remarkable migration.

Brian Harrington of the Manomet Bird Observatory holds a red knot that was captured three times in eleven months—in Massachusetts, in Argentina, and again in Massachusetts. This bird had covered nearly 20,000 miles.

Several minutes later Harrington says, "I think I have a green left, silver right." He is describing a bird wearing two bands, one colored green, the other a silver aluminum band with a number on it, supplied by the U.S. Fish and Wildlife Service. Leddy, without removing her eye from the scope, replies, "I think I just got that one. Silver lower right?" "Yeah," Harrington says. "That would be a bird we banded here a year ago." The unique band combination identifies where it was first handled and in what year. The information is not only useful for observing how birds from different areas mix, and establishing that they follow the same path year after year, but also for estimating how many knots there are. It involves an obtuse algebra, which Harrington explained to me this way: "We know how many birds we've banded in a given year at a given place. For the following twelve months or so, when we look for bands, we count how many from a certain locality we see, and how many birds we see altogether. For these purposes, we assume that birds from different areas mix randomly on migration, and that none of the birds we banded died. So, we set up a proportion just like they teach you in the seventh grade: The number of bands seen is to the size of the flock as the total number of birds we've banded is to the entire knot population." It is with that arithmetic that they've come up with the working estimate of 200,000 North American red knots.

So this leg-watching, and the careful recording of ratios of banded to unbanded birds, will feed Harrington's calculus. "So far, we've averaged about one percent banded birds on this trip," he says. If we've seen about 15,000 birds today, that would mean . . .

The red knot is known to scientists as *Calidris canutus,* possibly named for a legend about the Danish King Canute, variously spelled Cnut or Knut; hence, perhaps, the English name. Or possibly it was named for its flight note: a low *knut.* The "red" comes from the reddish blush on its breast while in breeding plumage.

In eighteenth- and nineteenth-century America, shorebirds were ruthlessly hunted for the dinner pot. Ornithologists believe this hunting was responsible for depressing the populations of shorebirds even to the present day. Both sport and market hunters opened fire on them each migratory season. Because of the birds' dense flocks, their plump, meaty bodies, and the open terrain they occupied, one well-placed shot could fell a dozen of the birds; rows of hunters firing all day could kill thousands. John James Audubon himself observed such a spree, by French market gunners in Louisiana in 1821; he estimated that 40,000 plovers were killed in a single day.

The knot, being a chunky ten inches long and tending to form tight flocks, made an easy target. As evidenced by their springtime abundance in Cape May, their numbers have recovered. However, most ornithologists agree that the shorebird flocks we see today are only remnants of the clouds that once wheeled across the open, undeveloped shores of the Northeast.

The Manomet team's estimate of 200,000 knots presents them with a problem. For all the careful searching and counting that they and their cooperators have done along the eastern seaboard, they can account for only about 20,000 birds on the southward trip. That leaves the bulk of the knots unaccounted for—undetected by the International Shorebird Survey—until the huge winter gathering appears in southern Argentina. That has led the Manomet researchers to the speculation that most knots fly nonstop from the Arctic to South America.

"It's remarkable, but maybe we shouldn't be completely surprised," Harrington said. "You have to realize that the heavy hunting that went on in the States would have been a strong kind of natural selection against those birds that stopped off here, so apparently most fly straight down. We surmise that there may be a landfall on the northern coast of South America—because they don't get to Argentina until mid-October—but we haven't found it yet."

Hemisphere-hopping seems to be the red knot's extravagant way of moving between environments rich in food sources. The best place to start the story of their journeys is on their reproductive turf. The story, as put together by the Manomet team, goes like this:

Knots arrive at their breeding grounds, mostly on islands in northern Hudson Bay and the high Canadian Arctic, by early June and raise their young in about five weeks.

Like other Arctic-nesting birds, the knot has traded off a relatively short "growing season" for the benefits of nesting in an area of abundant biological productivity—a result of the long period of summer daylight, which feeds the plant life that nurtures the rest of the food chain. By the second week in July, thousands of knots, along with other shorebirds, congregate around the shore of James Bay, at the southern end of Hudson Bay, their first major staging area. Here they feast on small clams and crustaceans, building up fat reserves that will provide the fuel for migration.

By October, when knots begin arriving en masse on the lower Argentine coast, summer is creeping up on that hemisphere, and the same sort of biological bloom that enriched the Arctic is occurring. Around the shores of Tierra del Fuego are flat rocky plains known as the *restinga*, pockmarked with tidal pools and covered with mussels, the knot's dietary staple for the season.

For those knots that stop off on the way south, the major landfall is in late July to mid-August around Cape Cod Bay—the Manomet Bird Observatory's home territory—where they group in flocks of up to 5,000. Blue mussels, the same ones served *à la marinière* in restaurants, have spawned abundantly during the summer, and the mudflats are covered with "spat"—yearling mussels under an inch in size. The knots feed voraciously on the spat flats, ultimately denuding some of them. When the birds arrive they weigh 120 grams; when they leave they weigh 180, and some have swelled to more

than 200 grams—nearly a doubling of their body weight, mostly in fat. Said David Twichell, "If you doubled the weight of your Piper Cub, you'd have trouble getting off the ground."

The next stop is assumed to be in northern South America. From there the birds appear to fly across the Amazon Basin (there are few sightings around the rim of Brazil) and begin gathering on the coast of central Argentina in early October. By late October, most are in Tierra del Fuego.

For those southernmost birds, the journey north begins in mid-March, when they start trickling up the Argentine coast. The first staging area is Península Valdés, well known as a breeding ground for whales and as a reserve for Patagonian wildlife. Here the expansive Argentinian pampas give way to bluffs and vast mudflats, an ideal place for knots to collect, again in the thousands, to fatten up on small clams. (Mollusks eaten by knots, *mirabile dictu,* are swallowed whole; the shells are ground fine in the gizzard and emerge smoothly out the bird's other end.) All along the coast the knots are chased by peregrine falcons and other predators, and pursued flocks frequently take to the air in twisting maneuvers of escape. Recalled Linda Leddy: "I was standing on the flats when I thought I heard the roar of a freight train behind me. It took me a moment to realize there weren't any trains there. When I turned to look, I saw about fifteen hundred knots being chased by a peregrine. It was such a jarring sound, my reaction was to duck. I don't know if the acoustics are differ-

On the beach at Cape May, New Jersey, researchers pull a cloth over a rocket net that has covered both horseshoe crabs and knots that feast on their eggs. The cloth keeps the birds from struggling to get free.

ent there, or if the birds are flying faster, but I've never heard a flock sound the way it does at Valdés."

During the last week of April the birds head north, and they begin to be seen in numbers around the U.S. Atlantic Coast first in Georgia and the Carolinas. (One early May report from Georgia was of 12,000 knots flying by in just two hours.) Then, some 600 miles to the north, the next and last major stopover—Cape May and the horseshoe crabs.

We are on a different beach on Delaware Bay, adjacent to a vast marsh crisscrossed with new drainage ditches. A bulldozer has left mudflats in its wake, and they are covered with resting shorebirds. "I think the birds get full and they just can't eat any more, so they have to rest awhile," Harrington says. The real action is on the beach proper, where the tide is going out, leaving a rich deposit of eggs. Mary Niles—a trustee of the Manomet Bird Observatory—is with us and has scooped up a handful of detritus—the "wrack" at the high-tide mark—which is about 80 percent eggs. She is peering at them through a hand lens. "They look like heads of pins," she says, never at a loss for simile, "or the beads that form in minute tapioca." She's right. They are grayish-green imperfect spheres less than two millimeters in diameter. All of us are impressed by their abundance and laugh at the thought of trying to estimate how many eggs there are lying wasted (from the horseshoe crab's point of view) on the beach.

The eggs are not the only waste. The beach is also littered with horseshoe crabs that have been overturned by wavelets or the tide. Many are alive and will be rescued by the next tide, but others will perish. The urge to tip the crabs back upright is irresistible—a sort of thwarting of natural selection. In Harrington's point of view, however, it is an investment in their work: "This year's crab-tipping is next year's knot food." And food of a crucial kind.

From here, for most knots, it will be straight to James Bay, Canada, and then to the breeding grounds by the first week in June. At that time of year, there is often still snow on the ground, and limited food is available to the birds at first. So, the Manomet researchers believe, the energy reserves gathered at Delaware Bay may be crucial for laying eggs.

The implications of that become clear when Harrington puts it in vivid terms: "How well these horseshoe crabs in New Jersey lay their eggs may determine how successfully red knots in Arctic Canada can breed.

And that, two months later, could affect the numbers of mussels on flats in Massachusetts—and a few months after that, in Argentina." It is an observation not merely to be marveled at; of chief concern to the Manomet team are the conservation implications. Delaware Bay is one of the busiest oil-tanker ports in the world, and although there hasn't been a recent oil spill there in springtime, the evident risk presents interesting possibilities. For the knots, events 9,000 miles apart can affect the size of the population; at Cape May a disaster might affect a substantial portion of their population.

"Keep in mind," Harrington said, "that the peak numbers here may represent a third of the knots in North America. Now suppose there was some sort of environmental disturbance. Even if the knots—not to mention the thousands of other shorebirds—escaped direct damage, would it affect the food they depend on? And if so, would it affect their successful migration and breeding? We don't know the answers to these questions. We do know that migration is a finely tuned process, in harmony with other ecological events, so we can make educated guesses. It looks as though for shorebirds Cape May is a critical area."

"We're really just starting to define what a critical area is," Leddy said. "We aren't looking here at an endangered species like whooping cranes, but we are looking at a species for which very limited geographic areas are very important. It seems less emotional, certainly less exigent, than endangered species, but for conservation it may be just as important."

Cape May may now be the knot's safest haven. With growing evidence of the area's great importance—both from the Manomet team's research and that of J. P. Myers of the Philadelphia Academy of Sciences—the governors of New Jersey and Delaware in 1986 named Delaware Bay a migratory shorebird reserve. The declaration carries no official weight, but Harrington hopes that in calling attention to Delaware Bay the declaration will help government and private conservation agencies make their cases for saving important parts of the shoreline, and perhaps even reduce the risk of industrial contaminations.

So in some minimal sense, Cape May is on the road to preservation. But at each of the other points in its migration route, the red knot illustrates the concept of "critical area," for it encounters hazards linked to modern technology, and peculiar to shorebirds' dependency on small parts of the Earth:

√ Massachusetts: Most of the beaches where knots congregate are privately owned, available for development, and heavily used for recreation right at the time the knots are there. Since the birds are especially sensitive to disturbance from people, the researchers fear that unregulated use of those sites poses a threat.

✓ Florida: knots have always used a single stretch of beach, between Naples and St. Petersburg, where a large disjunct group of wintering birds spends several months. The same stretch is being heavily developed. Knots are restricted to four small areas, some of them adjacent to condominiums and resorts.

✓ Northern South America: Subsistence hunting of migrating shorebirds and seabirds is carried on routinely; the birds are usually transfixed at night with lights and then netted. South American countries are also developing coastal oil reserves, presenting the possibility of an environmental accident.

✓ Argentina: A rapidly growing oil industry is changing the habitat available to shorebirds. Supertanker traffic that can't go through the Panama Canal goes around Cape Horn, passing the shorebird wintering grounds. And Península Valdés has been considered as the site of a tidal hydroelectric power station.

Beyond all this, knots exemplify a general issue of growing concern to American conservationists. For years, environmental protection for birds has focused on the breeding habitat. As important as that is, it accommodates just a short part of a migratory bird's annual cycle. What happens on the southern wintering grounds or at migration staging areas may offset the conservation efforts in the north. So in the case of migratory hawks, the concerns turn toward pesticide exposure in Latin America; with forest-dwelling birds, toward habitat destruction. And in the case of shorebirds, it has spawned the concept of an international system of "Sister Reserves"—critical staging areas preserved as sanctuaries, of which Delaware Bay is the first to be recognized. These become sensitive political issues that run across political boundaries. In modern conservation, they may be crucial for species preservation.

And of what use is such preservation? Like many other biologists, Brian Harrington reverts to philosophy when grappling with this. "There is wildlife with which we *must* share this planet, and we're just learning how to do that," he says. "Beyond that, there is something exciting about learning these things. It makes our world more interesting

to know that here's a bird, barely larger than a robin, that routinely migrates from one end of the globe to the other, that eats enough food to double its weight in ten or twelve days, that flies nonstop for several thousand miles and loses that weight. We're concerned about that bird's vulnerability, and we're trying to learn enough to know what to do about it."

Harrington's concern echoes one of nearly a century ago, yet it has a uniquely modern, perplexing edge. In 1897, a Massachusetts outdoorsman and diarist named George MacKay was moved to comment on the vacant stretch of beach he saw at Massachusetts Bay, once teeming with migratory shorebirds. Though he was himself an enthusiastic and ruthless hunter, MacKay wrote in an article in *The Auk,* "Are we not approaching the beginning of the end?" Observing in middle age the diminution of birds so plentiful in his youth, MacKay realized that the birds couldn't withstand unchecked hunting. He became a champion of laws against spring shooting to protect the breeding stock on its way north. In 1916, the Migratory Bird Treaty Act took shorebirds off the game lists permanently.

Thus were shorebirds protected from the technology of ordnance. In MacKay's time the conservation problem seemed clear and the solution easy. In Brian Harrington's time, the problems are larger, the solutions diffuse, the future unclear.

These knots on the beach at Siesta Key, near Sarasota, Florida, have been banded and flagged. Others were dyed yellow for easy spotting by researchers. The dye wears off in just a month or two.

WHEN THE ROADRUNNER NESTS

TEXT BY GEORGE LAYCOCK · PHOTOGRAPHY BY WYMAN P. MEINZER JR.

The roadrunner, or chaparral cock, known in Mexico as *paisano,* is an unlikely mixture of feathers and appetite. Lizards are a favorite food, and any lizard darting from the shadow of a rock or cactus may have a roadrunner in full pursuit.

The roadrunner, dashing off on long legs and counterbalancing on the sharp turns with its eleven-inch-long tail, overtakes the frantic lizard and whacks it on the head. Then it beats its victim on the ground, or pounds its head repeatedly against a nearby rock before swallowing it head-first.

During the roadrunner's nesting season, more than ever, lizards should lie low. Parent birds scour the countryside for lizards to keep their nestlings fed.

If the prey is a snake, the tail, complete with rattles, may dangle from the roadrunner's bill for a while until digestion clears room for it.

Even scorpions, centipedes, tarantulas, and horned lizards, armored and puffed up to fearsome proportions, are not safe from the roadrunner. Mice, baby birds, and car-

rion are all delicacies, and grasshopper hunting seems to combine pursuit of food with fun and games. The roadrunner stirs the grasshoppers into flight, then leaps wildly to snatch them from mid-air.

At other times, the hungry chaparral cock has its beady eye on sparrows. The bird moves casually until a careless sparrow passes close overhead. Then, leading the prey like a trained wingshot, the roadrunner bounds into the air and snatches the smaller bird.

Although rats approach the upper limit in prey size, they are not ignored. The late artist-ornithologist George Miksch Sutton once described how his two pet roadrunners dealt with a cotton rat that periodically scurried across a gap in the stone wall behind his Texas home. The roadrunners became increasingly interested in the travels of the rat and began loitering near the wall.

One day Sutton heard the rat squealing in terror and ran to the scene to find the rodent trying in vain to elude two lightning-quick roadrunners who, according to Sutton, "never really held him but pinched him,

Left, a roadrunner brings a Texas spotted whiptail to its nest, and below swallows a collared lizard head-first.

This roadrunner is shown on the run with a Texas horned lizard.

tossed him, dealt him blows, buffeted him, and made him weary with fighting for life." When the two birds could not decide who got the dead prize, and both attempted vainly to consume it from opposite ends, Sutton cut the rat in half for them.

The roadrunner is a member of the cuckoo family and lives in the desert scrub from central California to central Mexico and east into Arkansas and Louisiana. It spends much of its time on the ground, for it is better qualified as a runner than a flier. If pressed it will fly for short distances, but it can usually escape predators by running at speeds of more than fifteen miles an hour, or by hiding in the shadows of cholla, ocotillo, and thorn trees.

Wherever the roadrunner lives, it attracts attention for its appearance as well as its habits. It is the clown of the desert. One naturalist claims that the roadrunner looks like the early discarded doodling of a chicken designer. Two feet long and brownish in color, it has a body streaked with white and buff and is lighter on the underside. But these colors have iridescent undertones and may change with the light. The head carries a large blue-black crest, and there are bare patches of blue and orange skin behind the eyes.

Although seldom praised for the beauty of its song, a courting roadrunner will perch on a cactus at sunrise and sing a series of monotonous dove-like notes for an hour or more.

As a nest-builder, the roadrunner lacks the skills of the orioles and barn swallows. Its nest is a loose arrangement of sticks, perched in a tree or bush three to fifteen feet above the ground. Here the female may deposit three to six chalky white eggs and begin incubating them before the clutch is completed. For this reason there may be eggs and young of various ages in the nest at the same time.

Unlike most baby birds, the nearly naked young have black skin, and this serves them well. During the cool desert nights they are kept warm by their parents, but with daylight the adult birds must leave in search of food.

Then the young ones turn to passive solar energy, exposing their dark backs and soaking up the early sun. Adults also warm their own bodies at the beginning of day, lifting their feathers and aligning their bodies with the sun's rays.

The roadrunner may be a favorite cartoon character, but not everyone looks upon it with amusement. While it subsists largely on reptiles, insects, and arachnids, it is sometimes condemned for taking an occasional quail egg or nestling. This has, at times, put the roadrunner's name onto the list of the bountied species. What an ignoble end for the little *paisano*.

III
INSECTS AND SUCH

WOLF
OF THE SANDS

PHOTOGRAPH BY JOHN SHAW

On a beach along the south shore of Lake Superior, a "bank wolf" *(Arctosa littoralis)* crouches motionless under the midsummer sun. Its pale, mottled color makes it all but invisible against a variegated background of sand grains. Although *Arctosa* is a voracious predator in its own right, this camouflage serves to protect it from hunters larger than itself. These spiders seldom go abroad during the day but hide under driftwood or, occasionally, in a burrow that the spider digs in the sand. It does most of its hunting under cover of darkness, running nimbly over the sand in pursuit of insects and smaller spiders. Like other nocturnal members of the wolf spider family, it is easy to find if you have a flashlight, because its eight eyes glow brightly in reflected light. One of about twenty species of *Arctosa* spiders, *littoralis* is found only on beaches, stream banks, and in other sandy places. It ranges over much of the United States and southern Canada and is even found on sandy shores along the Atlantic Coast.

THE JOY OF BUTTERFLYING

TEXT BY ROBERT MICHAEL PYLE · PHOTOGRAPHY BY BECKY AND GARY VESTAL

A butterfly passes by, and few heads turn. Usually true, and a great pity. Most people's eyes are simply not open to anything smaller than a robin; their senses are not adjusted to take in small wonders. Even naturalists tend to be attuned to the greater spectacles, to the exclusion of the lesser. As Vladimir Nabokov observed in his memoirs, "It is astonishing how few people notice butterflies." Yet those who miss butterflies miss one of the greatest spectacles of all, in sheer wonder and beauty if not in size.

Few other subjects in the realms of nature or craft offer the degree of esthetic pleasure to be gained from butterflies. In a jaded, tiring world, butterfly watching furnishes a free and easy pathway to fascination and refreshment. Not an escape, but a fresh kind of connection with reality, butterfly watching provides a new nature alternative.

Seeking out and observing butterflies gives one a unique window on the world. One cannot become a butterfly lover without at the same time growing sensitive to animals, plants, soils, landforms, weather and climate, and the habitats they all make up together. So the watcher of butterflies soon becomes botanist, geologist, reader of clouds—in fact, a general naturalist. I know of few pursuits out-of-doors that lead one quite as a matter of course down so many avenues of nature. And this means that the lepidopterist gains as well an appreciation for the landscape as a whole, and an understanding of the imperative for thoughtful and caring land stewardship.

Perhaps I have made it sound as if you cannot participate in this activity without energetically pursuing a dozen others as well, when all you wanted to do was watch a butterfly, purely and simply. Actually, butterflying can be as rigorous or as gentle as you wish to make it. An example from the birthplace of butterfly studies, Great Britain, will illustrate this point. For the past decade I have been fortunate to live in England much of the time and therefore have done a lot of

my butterfly watching there. One would think that all challenges entomological would long since have been met in this small, well-inspected land, and that butterfly research would have run out of field problems to solve. Such is not at all the case. Much remains to be learned, particularly of species rare and becoming rarer; and despite the great British butterfly mapping system, Britain's wilder landscapes still hold some secrets and physical challenges for the field lepidopterist.

So it was that on a July day in 1972 I found myself in pursuit of the heath fritillary in northwest Devon. My survey of this threatened species presaged an intensive program for its study and recovery which is still going on. But I was then tracking down old known localities to discover whether the small orange-and-black brocade butterfly still occupied any of its former domains. On a hot, crystalline morning I struck up a steep slope, bound for a moor purple with heather and overlooking the Irish Sea, buoyant with hope and exhilaration. An hour later I was deeply enmeshed in the worst brier patch I ever hope to see from the inside—sixteen species of thorns, brambles, and stickers conspired to make my gentle Devon ramble into the worst outdoor ordeal I have ever experienced, New Guinea swamps and North Sea storms notwithstanding. I emerged very scratched up and bloody, none the wiser about the heath fritillary and seriously doubting the sensibility of my expedition. It had been an adventure one could appreciate only in retrospect.

Yet last spring, I experienced another English butterfly viewing of the most serene and mild kind. Seated on a white lawn chair in the garden of a Cambridgeshire pub on a golden May day, pint of fine East Anglian ale in hand and in a state of utter repose, I watched a brimstone flutter into the scene. The lemon-yellow butterfly dallied among the nectarless blossoms of like-colored daffodils and mauve crocuses. A fruitless foray

Milbert's tortoise shell (Nymphalis milberti): *"Butterflying can be as intellectually demanding as you wish."*

Common sulphur (Colias philodice), *above, and a mourning cloak* (Nymphalis antiopa), *right, sunning on a vine maple.*

for the butterfly perhaps, but a rich and memorable experience for me.

Likewise, butterflying can be as intellectually demanding as you wish, or you can approach it strictly on a basis of appreciation. The study of butterflies has led to enlightenment on matters medical, genetic, behavioral, and ecological, and prompted major strides in evolutionary understanding. For the perpetrators of this research, such as Professors Sir Cyril Clarke and Paul Ehrlich, the contemplation and observation of butterflies provided scientific grist no less stimulating or rewarding than the most arcane atomic particles or stellar phenomena. Meanwhile, poets have always approached butterflies on an emotional level, where the feelings they inspire mean as much as the facts they convey. This *gestalt* or zen level of butterfly appreciation is available to anyone willing to contradict that scientist–poet, Nabokov, and notice butterflies. For most of us, butterfly watching means something in between: a chance to sharpen our powers of observation, to learn something new and intriguing, while feeling good about and because of what we are doing.

A birder with whom I once discussed butterfly watching scoffed at the idea. "Butterflies are only there to watch in summer," he claimed, "whereas birds are always around." How wrong he was. Their active, adult flight extends in the North from early spring to late autumn, while in the South butterflies fly year-round. Even in the cold northern winters, mourning cloaks and their hibernating relatives may come out on sunny, snowy days. And of course paying attention to butterflies means, in the broader sense, being aware as well of their eggs, caterpillars, and chrysalids—the whole life cycle of the most remarkable changelings on Earth. Seeking or keeping the early stages in winter can make these creatures for all seasons.

"Well, then," countered the skeptical birder, "what about geography? I can find birds in any habitat—surely butterflies hang out in few places other than flowery meadows?" Wrong again. The only bird habitats devoid of butterflies are open water and the Antarctic. And even open water must be qualified—Columbus and Darwin and many others since have reported great clouds of sulphurs far out at sea. Butterflies have come to dwell in virtually every terrestrial habitat except icefields. Indeed, they are at least as abundant and diverse as birds in rigorous habitats such as the High Arctic, the Arctic–Alpine, and the desert.

"And weather?" He was flagging. It is true enough that butterflies strongly prefer sunny weather, while clouds put down many species even on warm days. Butterfly watching in the rain tends to be a fairly futile experience. But even then, as in winter, caterpillars are abroad on the land. And locating the resting place of a sheltered butterfly in a thundershower, beneath a leaf or deep in mountain turf, is a magical experience; what it lacks in frequency it makes up in fulfillment.

"Surely," he parried his last, "you can't find butterflies at night? At least we can prowl for owls and nightjars in the wee hours." I told him about zebra butterflies, which roost communally in Florida and may be found in their striking, striped nocturnal assemblages with the aid of a flashlight, or by watching them bed down at dusk. I mentioned crepuscular nymphs in New Guinea that I watched well into the tropic twilight, and night-feeding fritillary larvae that come out to browse on violets only after the sun goes down. If that's not enough for the night-person, consider moths, butterflies' counterparts of the shadow-world. Moths number among them many beauties. They are mostly nocturnal and at least ten times more numerous and diverse as the dryads of

A monarch, left, on a Monterey pine, waits out a shower. Below, an Acmon blue (Plebejus acmon) and, right, a Zerene fritillary (Speyeria zerene) attest that butterflies "are as colorful and many-patterned as flowers yet obviously more active. And they are as fascinating as birds in their behavior but much easier to approach and watch close-up."

the daylight. And one more thing. With butterflies, you needn't make excuses for missing that five o'clock field trip: Unlike birds, they begin their day's activity at the very civilized hour of eight or nine o'clock.

The birder was beaten. He has since become an avid butterfly watcher and finds that butterflies and birds complement each other nicely as field pursuits. In fact, a number of National Audubon Society chapters now stage butterfly field trips annually or even more often: I led Seattle Audubon's first such walk on May Day, 1970, and they have proved popular ever since. Butterflies are not likely to edge out birds as the most watched creatures, but they have begun to be discovered and have not been found wanting.

It may be said that looking at butterflies is the least appreciated of the three great, colorful outdoor pleasures: watching birds, watching butterflies, and discovering wildflowers. In many ways, though, butterflies may be thought of whimsically as a mixture of the other two groups. They are not so bewilderingly various as wildflowers yet just as

diverse as birds in North America and more so worldwide. They are as colorful and many-patterned as flowers yet obviously more active. And they are as fascinating as birds in their behavior but much easier to approach and watch close-up. Hazel Wolf, doyenne of Seattle Audubon Society, has called butterflies "wildflowers with wings." They might as well be thought of as the birds of the invertebrate world. (Butterflies and birds even share the trait of having the female carry the sex-determining chromosome—unlike virtually all other animals!)

So while birdwatching and wildflower appreciation far outnumber butterflying in their devotees, birds and flowers offer no greater quality, color, or fascination. Perhaps their lead is owed in part to the fact that there are many more field guides on them, but that is less true today than it was a few years ago. Too, these other organisms are more conspicuous; often it takes a teacher or interpreter to point out butterflies at first.

I teach with butterflies—about the land, about biology, about the creatures them-

A western tiger swallowtail (Papilio rutulus) *embraces morning sunshine.*

selves and how they react to human uses of the world. One of my great pleasures is being able to extend someone's limited experience with butterflies, for these are not joys for the ablebodied alone. I have taught butterfly appreciation to the blind and disabled. The mere fact that I can do so signals that virtually everyone, some with a bit of help, can enjoy butterflies in their lives.

Even though butterfly "watching" can be done with fingers or smell, most of us are fortunate to be able to do so with sight. Yet observation in the strict sense only begins to suggest the pleasures that attention to butterflies can bring. Little photographed until recently, butterflies offer an incomparable array of color and form. Butterfly photography is challenging to say the least, but its satisfactions far outstrip its difficulty. Then there is the rearing of butterflies from eggs, larvae, or pupae. No other miracle in nature begins to approach, in my view, the sheer wonder of Lepidoptera metamorphosis. To see it happen before your eyes can be a transcendental experience. At the least, it is always deeply fascinating and satisfying.

Both gardeners and entomologists in England have long engaged in butterfly gardening, whereby the resources in the garden are carefully managed to lure and keep more butterflies than might otherwise come. New World gardeners are beginning to discover the delights of this practice.

Beyond watching, depicting, gardening, and rearing, some proportion of butterfly lovers will go on to sample and study their subjects in a scientific manner. This is not necessary in order to enjoy butterflies fully, but it is true that out of an early sense of wonder followed by open-eyed watching, many a biologist is born.

My own conversion to a butterfly watcher and biologist came early, but not before I'd sortied elsewhere with less than satisfying results. As a very young boy my strongest passions were reserved for two categories of things: seashells and suits of armor. Both commodities were singularly uncommon in my native Colorado. I kept my habits alive with fixes from shell shops, museums, and the printed page. Diminishing returns began to set in. Then one day while wandering in a raw new park near my suburban home, I spotted and wondered at some little whirring, bluish objects among the weeds. Later I found a brilliant butterfly, dead and dried with wings spread open, on a pitcher's mound in the same park. These harbingers turned out to be checkered skippers and a viceroy.

Soon I began to see great chocolate and va-

nilla mourning cloaks, salmon-spotted painted ladies, astonishing black swallowtails, and little blue butterflies ("Blue!" I thought) along the fencerows. It began to dawn on me that butterflies might provide a more fruitful field for a Denver lad than medieval armor or conchology. One day my stepbrother, Bruce Campbell, announced he was going to begin an insect collection. I offered to do the butterflies. So at age eleven I went afield along a local ditch with net in hand, and I've never looked back.

In the years that followed, my grandfather used to ask in jest if there was any money in butterflies. I doubted it, and I was mostly right. But butterflies have brought me a different kind of reward that I value much more. It is serenity, and it provides perhaps the best advertisement of all for becoming involved with butterflies. Personal peace is hard to find in the frenetic world we have made. Yet for me, no moments are more peaceful than those I spend among the butterflies, whether in Elysian fields or a vacant lot. And private peace translates into a wider peace, if enough people possess it. No butterfly lover ever started a war, to my knowledge. Without wishing to seem facetious, I commend spending time with the gentle, beguiling butterflies to anyone with tension to dissipate, stress to dispel, hostility to sublimate. Personal realities tend to prevent extended periods of communion with nature, and the gritty edges of modern life have a way of reimposing themselves. Yet those moments of peace and release are worth fortunes spent on pills, spas, doctors, and analysts.

I recall one particularly grueling international conservation meeting when I felt quite worn down by the concerns and conflicts involved. I fled for an afternoon's walk up a narrow valley above Lake Geneva. In a tiny Swiss meadow, an early April orange-tip wafted over pink cardamine, its host plant. I was able to coax the splendid, fresh insect onto my finger; not a scale was missing from its bright orange-and-linen wings. And not a care was present in that meadow, nor any longer in me. I returned from the meadow fully refreshed and reminded of the reasons for working to conserve such places for butterflies and people.

In a stress-ridden society, there are a thousand prescriptions for peace of mind. I have found nature study, and in particular the contemplation of butterflies, to be the best tonic in my own search for serenity. It is just as effective, incidentally, in banishing boredom. Butterflies are simply never boring.

IV
LIFE IN THE WATER

THE KELP SNAIL'S LIFE OF HARD LABOR

TEXT AND PHOTOGRAPHY BY CHUCK DAVIS

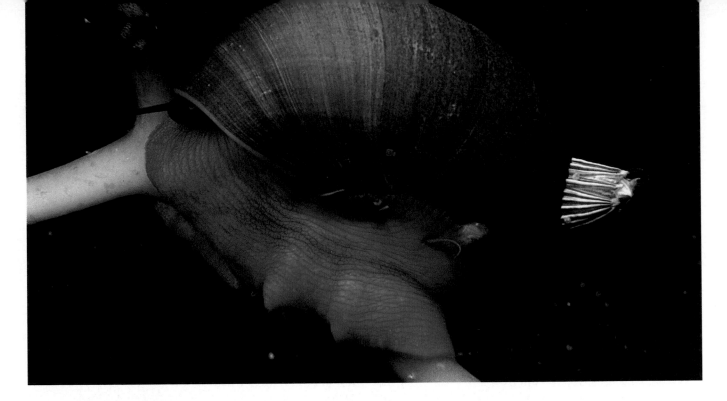

Easily recognized by its vibrant red mantle, the kelp snail, *Norrisia norrisi,* is one of the most colorful residents of the southern California kelp forests.

Also known as the smooth turban, Norris shell, and Norris' top snail, *Norrisia* can be found on the holdfast, stipe, and canopy of giant kelp plants as well as in the intertidal zone associated with other brown algae.

A mollusk and member of the gastropod class, this species is small in physical size (averaging approximately two inches in diameter) and feeds mainly on brown algae. Geographically, it occurs from Point Conception, California, southward to Baja, with a depth range that extends from the intertidal zone to nearly a hundred feet.

From a human standpoint, it would seem that *Norrisia* is doomed to a life of endless hard labor: After locating a kelp holdfast (the ball of leathery strands which holds the plant to the reef bottom) the snail begins an upward journey while it feeds on the kelp's surface-cells and micro-algae (a process that is reported to do little, if any, harm to a healthy kelp plant). Ultimately, if it is not shaken loose by currents or surface-wave action, the snail may make its way to the tip of a kelp blade and, as if walking the plank, fall off. Undaunted, it will tumble to the reef floor only to begin its upward climb all over again.

To the casual observer, *Norrisia's* feeding may appear to occur only in an upward direction, but experiments conducted in the kelp beds near Santa Catalina Island suggest that kelp snails (ones that must keep a better than average grip on the kelp) may follow a daily vertical migration pattern, traveling up during late afternoon and night and down during the day. Other biologists, however, feel that the snail's climbing is purely random, although possibly influenced by predation of starfish, crabs, lobsters, octopuses, and (according to one report) gulls, which can pluck the snails off in very shallow water.

If it can avoid a short list of predators, the kelp snail seems destined to live a simple life, required only to crawl, eat, and make more kelp snails.

Unlike its simple life-style, *Norrisia's* reproductive cycle is a bit more complex. This species reproduces sexually, with males and females giving off their sexual products into the sea. Fertilization results in what zoologists call a "veliger" larva. In contrast to its parents, the veliger is a free-swimming creature which does not even resemble an adult. Later, it will transform into a miniature snail and settle on the kelp forest floor to quite literally begin its climb through life.

As if carrying its own weight through life is not burden enough, *Norrisia* may play host to a menagerie of living organisms such as encrusting algae and barnacles which colonize the surface of its shell. Heavily encrusted individuals may take on a peculiar decorated appearance, resembling miniature reefs unto themselves.

However peculiar they may appear, their design must be a perfect one, for like all else in the sea forest, they would not exist if they were not champions in executing the purpose that nature has set down for them: Perhaps like Hemingway's Paris, they are the design for a movable feast.

LITTLE COUSIN OF THE LOBSTER

BY EDWARD O. WELLES

Louisiana is one state that ought, perhaps, to be two. Up north it is stolid, Baptist, meat-and-potatoes, piney-woods country. But as you head south, pines yield to hardwoods, Protestants to Catholics, and the stiff upper lip to *joie de vivre*. Down in south Louisiana, French is as apt to roll off a person's tongue as English. Down here, people take their sustenance from the myriad rivers and bayous that vein the land. This is Cajun country. Crawfish country.

Cajuns and crawfish seem virtually inseparable in south Louisiana. And as definitive of the region as anything else. Even their names are endemic. Up in Nova Scotia, whence the Cajuns came to Louisiana, they were known as Acadians. And crawfish are everywhere else known as crayfish; the local spelling and pronunciation have been made official by act of the state legislature.

Louisiana's Cajuns are of French–Catholic stock, and their taste for shellfish reaches back to the Old World. The Acadians settled eastern Canada early in the seventeenth century, but the French colony became English in 1713, part of the Treaty of Utrecht's settlement of Queen Anne's War. In 1755, during the French and Indian War, the British expelled all the Acadians who would not sign an oath of loyalty to the British crown—some six thousand men, women, and children. It has been suggested by some that the British also held against the Acadians their strange language, religion, and fondness for that detestable creature, the lobster.

In any event, the Acadians bumped on south through the American colonies, finding plenty of persecution as they went. In Louisiana, they finally found the tolerance they were looking for, as well as the familiar customs and culture of a former French colony. And, of course, the lobster's freshwater, look-alike, smaller cousin, the crayfish.

Until the late 1950s, the Cajuns and their south Louisiana neighbors had the crayfish pickings pretty much to themselves. But, with the oil boom, new people moved in, people who developed a taste for crayfish, but not the inclination to look for and catch them. So a commercial crayfish industry developed.

Today, it is a $30 million industry in Louisiana, which supplies about 98 percent of all the crayfish that Americans consume, and 88 percent of the catch is consumed inside Louisiana. New York and Texas are the only significant export markets so far, but others are developing.

But crawfishing isn't an industry like the oil industry. There are no crawfish magnates with expensively furnished boardrooms and private jets. It's a seasonal industry—from December into the summer—and even in season most of the commercial crawfishermen are part-timers. If it were possible to figure in all the crawfish that are sold from the back of trucks parked along the roadsides, some state fisheries people think the actual commercial catch might be a lot higher than the officially reported one—as much as three times higher, if all the crawfish taken for the family tables could be accounted for. So the millions of dollars get divided among thousands of Cajun crawfishermen, few of whom make more than a couple thousand dollars from the fishing. Virtually all of the wild crayfish harvest in Louisiana—as many as 24 million pounds or nearly 60 percent of the total catch, the balance coming mainly from commercial crayfish-culture ponds—are taken in the Atchafalaya Basin, a major distributary of the Mississippi. Into it spills nearly a third of the big river's flow. When the Mississippi floods each spring, the waters rise out of the Atchafalaya's channel and push back in against the levees that flank the 600,000-acre basin. This flooding opens the deepest chambers of the swamp to man. He lays out hand-fashioned, wire-mesh funnel traps baited with fish, chicken necks, beef spleen, cat food, corn on the cob, or almost any other sort of bait that comes to mind or hand.

Red crayfish, *Procambarus clarkii*, account for the bulk of the catch, about 90 percent.

In south Louisiana, Acadians and crayfish—more properly Cajuns and crawfish—are inseparable.

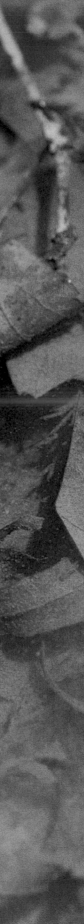

C.C. LOCKWOOD/BRUCE COLEMAN INC.

A hefty specimen will weigh about three ounces, but only the "tail" (actually the abdomen) is eaten. The "tail" accounts for about 15 percent of a crayfish's total weight. Most of the waste is discarded, dumped in landfills, or spread over pasturelands of fallow agricultural fields, but more beneficial uses are being studied.

As the floodwaters drop, the crawfishing season withers away. The crayfish follow the receding waters, burrowing down into the soil to find a new supply and to ready themselves for reproduction. Boats no longer can penetrate to the quick of the swamp. Summer is here. The season ends.

The seeds for a good spring harvest are sown in the other seasons. Ideally, summer should scorch the swamp, isolating pockets of water and robbing them of oxygen. This kills off the fish that prey on crayfish and replenishes protective vegetation. Autumn should be wet with rain, flushing the crayfish and their newborn young out of their burrows, reconnecting the swamp with oxygen-rich water. A good winter is a wet and mild one. Then this cold-blooded crustacean will have the impetus to feed, to grow, to fatten up for the spring kill.

To find the Atchafalaya, you head west out of Baton Rouge, crossing the high steel arch of a bridge over the Mississippi. Then you cut south, away from the surreal metalscapes of the riverbank refineries, and head out through the hot, low country that is spiked with sugarcane. The road winds on down to the bayou country and past little backwater towns with names like Plaquemine, Bayou Sorrel, Lone Star.

In Bayou Pigeon lives Gaulbert Hebert, a genial, robust Cajun who has spent all forty-five years of his life in this little bayou town. He has two boats in his garage and a restaurant that serves things like "turtle sauce picante" and crawfish bisque. The restaurant is a modest, cinderblock, hand-lettered-sign sort of place, and he was busy expanding it the warm spring day I visited. The restaurant stands only a foot above sea level; I remarked on this after he told me that standing water had kept it closed for five weeks earlier in the year.

Hebert leaned on his hammer and said, "Hey, man, have you ever seen a 'coon ass' want to be dry? We make our living wet." Originally a pejorative, "coon ass" was a term reserved for Cajuns who left the swamps and found work on the east Texas oil rigs. Now, though, it is a badge of pride among people who hold fast to their culture, who still speak French as their first language. Today, a coon ass is someone like Hebert whose formal education ended with grade school, but whose schooling in the basin is doctoral in depth.

Except for the three days each week that he opens the restaurant, Hebert spends virtually all of his time back in the basin, bringing out what his wits, his boats, and the law allow

him. "Nobody knows the crawfish," he says. "If they tell you they do, they're lying." Some years the water will be high, but the catch low. Where they will gather in the basin from year to year is a mystery. Hebert searches for signs: blackbirds that orient to crayfish breeding grounds, night herons that thrive on them, shoals of feeding fish.

Amidst this fathomless faunal ebb and flow stands a less oblique symbol, the oil well. Hebert says that drillers go into the basin, dig a "location," and throw up spoil that blocks the current and creates pools of stagnant water. "That's dead water back in there," he says. "How are your crawfish going to live in that? These oil companies don't care. The wildlife is catching hell in there."

Hebert recalled that twenty-five years ago he could go out and catch eight hundred pounds of crayfish a night. "We were getting four cents a pound then; we thought that was a lot." Now crayfish sell for as much as a dollar a pound. There are more people fishing the basin, and fewer crayfish to go around. Now, Hebert says, people descend on pockets of crayfish "like buzzards on a dead cow."

A friend stops by, wanting to sell Hebert a load of turtles out of Arkansas. Hebert leans on his hammer and considers. "I believe I'll take 'em." He explains that this species has been scarce in the basin of late and that "they sure do make good soup." As for crabs, though, "the last few years they've come back. Hell, they must've stayed away for ten or twelve years." He shakes his head and returns to hammering. "Can't figure it."

Mindful of the quiet anguish of men like Hebert who rely on the Atchafalaya Basin full-time for a living, the state in November 1981 announced a plan to better protect this resource. A compromise was forged which sought to end a decade of wrangling between environmentalists, fishermen, landowners, oil interests, and the Army Corps of Engineers. Under the plan, landowners would sell 50,000 acres of basin land to the state, and Dow Chemical would make an outright

gift of 50,000 acres. This would increase state ownership of the basin—and thus public access—from 140,000 to 240,000 acres. The state would seek "habitat preservation easements" from private landowners on the remaining 60 percent of the 600,000-acre basin. Landowners, though, would retain mineral, timber, and public-access rights. Oil and gas exploration would be permitted.

Though this compromise has enjoyed substantial local support, it continues to lack for one notable ingredient—money. "That's a real problem," says Oliver Houck, a law professor at Tulane who was instrumental in putting the plan together. To preserve the Atchafalaya, he believes, it would take between $100 and $150 million. The most logical source for that kind of money—in an austere, illogical time—is the federal government. Says Houck, "We've run into an administration that's death on funding anything beyond defense. I see aggressive hostility in this administration toward any program dealing with the environment."

And time is of the essence, according to Baton Rouge Audubon Society's Charles Fryling: "Those easements have got to be acquired now to ensure the integrity of the floodplain and the maintenance of the basin's unique natural environment."

In 1985 the state of Louisiana went out and bought 16,000 acres in the basin, in order to induce the federal government to act. It still hasn't. "It took from 1981 when we cut this deal to 1985 for Congress, over the administration's resistance, to authorize the plan. And now the administration, having lost the battle on authorization, is stonewalling the appropriation process," says

Left: A crayfish constructs its burrow. The female will drive the male from the burrow at egg-laying time. Below: A female carries several hundred fertilized eggs. Immediately after fertilization, the eggs are attached to swimmerets beneath the abdomen. The female must keep the eggs wet at all times to enable oxygen to diffuse from the atmosphere of the burrow into the developing embryos. The young crayfish are 1/3 inch long when they leave their mother.

Gaulbert Hebert launches his pirogue: "Nobody knows the crawfish. If they tell you they do, they're lying."

Houck, who would like to persuade those holding the purse strings that preserving the basin amounts to more than just saving a swamp. "If this administration is going to believe in flood control, then sooner or later they're going to have to do it in the Atchafalaya." Doing so, he says, would provide "an enormous dividend," crayfish. "These are big dollars down here. Crayfishing is an industry as well as a way of life."

But man's ways of life must ultimately dance to higher tunes, and it is safe to assume that the basin's shape in the years ahead will be forged by forces more surpassing than money.

Prime among these is the Mississippi River.

Think of the lower Mississippi River over the eons as a loose hose packed with pressure, spraying fitfully around a semicircular arc. Never is it still. There are five identifiable lower channels of the river in Louisiana. Right now it wants to jump and seize the Atchafalaya as its main passage to the Gulf of Mexico. It wants to shift course and pour on through the basin. Thus far, man has denied the river.

In 1963, the Army Corps of Engineers completed a water-control structure designed to send—into perpetuity—about 70 percent of the Mississippi's flow down the main channel, while spilling the rest through the Atchafalaya Basin. This ensured that enough freshwater would flow past New Orleans and Baton Rouge to keep saltwater from invading the channel. Those port cities are home in a big way to this country's vast petrochemical industry, which won't run on saltwater.

Raphael Kazmann, a hydrological engineer at Louisiana State, says, "You can't stabilize the river. Geomorphologically, this is the most active area in the country. It's like one big funnel for all that water. Anyone building a structure here and expecting it to last is out of his mind." Furthermore, says Kazmann, when the Corps built the water-control structure they created a "ferocious political problem"—compromise plan or no compromise plan. "There is not enough water to go around during dry periods," he says. Industry on the main channel needs water and fears floods, but fishermen and environmentalists want to see the basin remain "wet and wild." In wet years there is the persistent prospect of flood.

At present, about 30 percent of the big river's flow comes through the basin, and at times that is not enough for those who depend on it. Upstream, the Atchafalaya River is cutting a deeper channel and draining swampland—something man was never able to do. Meanwhile, downstream, where the basin widens, the river loses its pace and drops its considerable load. The Mississippi drains 41 percent of the conterminous United States, the heart of America, where today the Dust Bowl seems a dim memory and soil conservation is a lost art. Topsoil washes off fields in Iowa, Indiana, Tennessee; the soil is carried down the Mississippi, which connects to the Atchafalaya. It is here, in the muddy, opaque waters of the basin, that you find the lifeblood of America's farms. "The basin is silting in in back, and the water lacks force to get back in there and clean the swamp out. There's a lot of bad water now." This is Jim Voisin speaking, and the bad, oxygenless water he refers to means fewer crayfish. Voisin is thirty-five, and the wide-open basin he recalls as a youth has come to be studded with sandbars that give root to water-loving willows. Established hardwoods, meanwhile, die, their roots smothered by sand. Voisin's parents grew up in the basin, the only people on an eighty-acre island. "They didn't know what the Depression was," he says. When they needed cash they picked Spanish moss for furniture stuffing, earning a nickel a pound. There was a big oak tree on the island, and from a branch of it hung a swing. "When I was little, that branch was twenty-five feet in the air. The last time I went back in there and found it, I had to bend over to get under it."

There is corroboration of what Voisin says a few miles down the road from Hebert's restaurant, in the town of Pierre Part. There Mike Blanchard stands under a tin roof out of the midday sun. The tools of his trade—telephone, scale, small refrigerated truck—are all around him. Blanchard is a crayfish buyer, a man who chews toothpicks and looks perpetually worried. "This is a fast business. You're dealing with a perishable you've got to move every day. You can lose your shirt if you don't know what you're doing."

Last year, he says, he could count on 15,000 pounds of crayfish a day. "This year you might buy eight thousand one day, then only two thousand the next. The fishermen have had to move around a lot; they've had to set two sets of traps." Now and again the hot stillness out on the road is broken by a crayfisherman pulling up in a pickup and

EDWARD O. WELLES

hefting a few fifty-pound onion sacks onto Blanchard's scale. From there they go into a stack against the back wall of the shed, and the sound of crayfish clawing, gasping—their gills still wet—is a strangely soothing one. It is like the patter of rain on a sidewalk. Blanchard looks over his shoulder at the stacks of crayfish, bagged either in red or purple sacks. He says, "Them crawfish look pretty in those purple sacks, don't they?" He is right. They seem to shimmer.

Buyer and seller exchange money and conversation. Notes are folded and tucked into shirt pockets while there is talk that this might be it for this season. There is some shaking of heads. It is only late May; the season should really go another three weeks. Another pickup comes in, a boat in its bed. "Hey, you got your pirogue out." The reference is to the traditional narrow wooden boat Cajuns used to use before the age of Evinrude and Mercury. It is useful for getting back into the crevices of a swamp where outboard power won't take you, where maybe a few more crayfish are hiding.

Now another man pulls up. He is grimfaced, a buyer from across the basin in the town of Breaux Bridge, where the silting problem has been acute. He and Blanchard talk perfunctorily, with little warmth. They shift from English to French and back again, a linguistic sparring of sorts. The man leaves, saying he will check back on his return up the road. Blanchard grunts, turns, and says, "He wanted to buy some crawfish from me. I don't like to say nothing in front of him, but why should they get all this publicity when they have to come over here and take our crawfish?" As Blanchard explains, Breaux Bridge calls itself the crawfish capital of the

Above: A baited crayfish trap. Below left: Fred. Kyle with a three-ounce Atchafalaya giant. "It used to be I'd go out in the marsh, and I'd never see another person unless I was looking for them. Now there's more people and less swamp."

DONALD M. BRADBURN

97

world—officially, *"La Capitale de Mondiale des Ecrevisses"*—and its annual festival draws some hundred thousand visitors.

On balance, the last thirty years in south Louisiana have been abnormally dry, leading to stagnant water and a receding fear of flood. One inevitable year in the future, the Mississippi will rise up and run towns like Breaux Bridge right off the map. But for now, concerns are more immediate, specifically those centering on the steadily rising demand for crayfish.

Nowadays, restaurateurs in such exotic places as New York are ringing up Louisiana and ordering crayfish by the ton, at six dollars a pound and up. To meet this demand, more and more of the crop is being "farmed." Currently, some 60,000 acres of crayfish-culture ponds account for about 40 percent of the state's annual yield. Steve Afeman says, "I think the local market will eventually fade out in the basin. They're getting more and more bad water in there. We've had fishermen tell us this year they couldn't get back into where they had been fishing before. If you don't have ponds to support your plant, you'll be in trouble."

Afeman manages a crayfish-peeling plant near the town of Franklin for a man named Fred. Kyle, who shares Afeman's belief that the way to go is to set up a crayfish island empire that encompasses ponds and plant. "When the basin comes in I won't need it," Kyle says. "I'm taking steps to survive. I won't have to fool with anybody else."

Kyle says that with a smile. He is a crusty man whose pet peeve seems to be the human race. Most arresting about him are his eyes, milky blue sapphires set in a face burned red and leathery by sixty-three years in the sun. They seem animal. His grandfather was a riverboat captain who came down here and stayed, buying up timberland along the way. Kyle grouses about the basin's turning into a "mudpie." But he also says: "You're faced with a choice. You destroy New Orleans or you destroy the basin before its time. There's a multibillion-dollar industrial complex down there. No one's going to let that go under."

An outpost of that industrial complex—a powerplant—shimmers on the horizon in the late day's sun. Fred. Kyle, standing amidst his crayfish ponds, jerks his thumb over his shoulder at it and says, "Civilization." Then he points in the opposite direction at dense, wooded swamp: "Wilderness. And in the middle here, crawfish. The birds get some, and I get some. We got a good deal going." These broad, shallow ponds are where Kyle spends his days, doing his best to imitate nature, keeping the water moving, draining the ponds at certain times of the year.

As we walk around them the talk soon lapses from crayfish. Kyle talks about wolves, birds, and alligators, and how he wants this place to be a refuge for animals. He cannot disguise his glee as he shows off big, unworried alligators lurking in his ponds and rolling their marble eyes at us. Some people say that if the panther is making a stand in these parts he is doing it somewhere back in deep on Fred. Kyle's land.

Later, after dinner, Kyle will confide that as a young man he "was like everyone else. I shot anything that moved. Now I just want to look." He will squint his magical blue eyes at the past and say: "It used to be I'd go out in the marsh, and I'd never see another person unless I was looking for them. We were operating on the edges of where these animals lived. A few would wander out, and we'd take them. But they had their breeding grounds way back in the middle of the swamp. Now there's more people and less swamp, and we're going right into the heart of where these animals breed."

Kyle, the crusty sentimentalist, nonetheless knows what side his bread is buttered on—that of innovation and progress. He was the first processor around to install a peeling machine. The crayfish travel on conveyor belts that lead through rollers that look like wringers on old washing machines, then move through a gentle cooking and from there are frozen in plastic bags.

When Kyle put in the machine it displaced sixty-five workers. Many were diligent folk who also knew—after decades of war—what displacement meant. So they went up the road to Seafood, Inc., in Henderson and hired on there. Bobby Guidry and Charlie Friedman run that plant, and they proudly take me back into its bowels. Along tables piled high with crawfish stand many of Kyle's former labor force: Vietnamese of both sexes and all ages, wearing baseball-type caps advertising farm machinery and fertilizer. The Vietnamese family in full extension. "We pay by piecework," says Friedman; "a person can make $200 to $400 a week."

Says Guidry, "These people are like we were thirty years ago, when we needed to work to live. They aren't spoiled by the American ways, you know. They come in at three or four in the morning if you need them." Adds Friedman, "They're more work-conscious, more money-conscious. You can't have some of your workers going home at two in the afternoon and expect to run a business. They cost us more than American labor because we help them with their rent. But, for the peace of mind to know they'll be there next morning, it's worth it."

Vietnamese workers, peeling machines, silt in the basin; all are portents of a change in a livelihood, in a tradition, that dates back to when white men came to settle their ways upon the country. But it's a tradition that will die hard.

Each spring, when crayfish are most plentiful, crawfish boils highlight the Louisiana social calendar the way clambakes do in New England and barbecues do out West. But each has its own special flavor. To quote from a publication of the Louisiana State University Center for Wetland Resources, "The crawfish are boiled in salty, well-seasoned water along with potatoes, corn on the cob, sausages, and artichokes. The standard serving is about five pounds (one hundred crawfish) per person." Tradition, and the spiciness of the cooking water, require that equally prodigious quantities of beer be consumed.

The crawfish boil I attended was held under a spreading live oak in the shadow of the state capitol in Baton Rouge. It had been thrown for other state representatives by C. J. "Judge" Russo Jr., who had introduced a bill that would name the town of Pierre Part the crawfish capital of the *universe*.

People gather at a crawfish boil to affirm not only a regional but a human tradition. In the lee of the ritual there is plenty of time for conversation, for sharing concerns and retouching the bases of kinship and friendship. Oudrey Gros is in his mid-twenties. Between hefting tubs of fiery red crayfish into vats of steamy, spicy water, he talks about the basin that has been his backyard all his years. "The oil companies cut these canals into the basin. That gives more access into your hidden spots. Now everyone can get there. It used to be that I'd go out and get my eight squirrels every year. Now if I get eight, I'm proud."

Gros speaks flawless French, seasoned liberally with Cajun idiom. This is a hidden linguistic spot the mass culture has yet to cut a canal to. I ask him about this. "I love both languages," he says. "I wouldn't give either away. When you talk to the old people they relate to you a lot better if you speak French. They respect you for it." Cajuns lose their French, he feels, not when they go and take work on the outside but through "laziness in the home," when a parent simply doesn't make the effort to teach the child. "My wife and I—she's pregnant, gonna have a baby in two months—we're absolutely determined that baby's gonna speak French. The way we see it, you lose your French and you lose your Cajun heritage." Some would say he might as well have been talking about crayfish. Only, they'd have said "crawfish."

CRAYFISH DELIGHTS

SOUTHERN LIVING

EDWARD O. WELLES

BOILED CRAYFISH

Into a large pot, pour enough cold water to cover crayfish. To each quart of water, add ½ cup salt, 2 slices lemon, 2 whole allspice, 1 sliced onion, 1 sprig thyme, 1 bay leaf, 1 red pepper pod, ¾ teaspoon celery seed, and ½ teaspoon black pepper. (If you wish, you may use 2 tablespoons of commercial crab boil seasoning instead.) Note: Do not decrease amount of salt; water must be briny.

Bring seasoned water to boil, and boil 10 minutes. Add live crayfish. Return to boil. After crayfish have risen to surface and then sunk again, turn off heat. Let crayfish steep in hot water 10 minutes. Drain. Serve hot or cold with cold beer and crackers.

CRAYFISH JAMBALAYA

2 lbs. crayfish tails, peeled

2 tbsp. cooking oil

2 medium onions, chopped

3 shallots, chopped

2 cloves garlic, chopped

¼ cup snipped parsley

1 cup uncooked rice

2 cups water

¼ tsp. cayenne

1 tbsp. salt

In a heavy pot, cook onions, shallots, and garlic in oil over low heat about 10 minutes, stirring constantly. Add crayfish, salt and cayenne and cook about 15 minutes more over medium heat. Spoon out crayfish and most of the vegetables. Add rice to pan drippings and stir to coat well. Add water and ½ teaspoon salt. Cover and cook over low heat 20 minutes. Uncover and add cooked crayfish mixture and parsley. Cook about 15 minutes more. Serves 4.

CRAYFISH ETOUFFEE

1 lb. peeled crayfish tails

1 cup white onions, finely chopped

1 cup celery, with leaves, finely chopped

½ cup green onions, finely chopped

½ cup parsley, snipped

1 stick butter

Over medium heat, sauté white onions and celery in butter about 20 minutes, until translucent. Add green onions and parsley and cook 10 minutes more. Season to taste. Add crayfish and cook 8 minutes, until tails curl. Serve over hot rice. Serves 3 or 4.

THE NATURE OF CRAYFISH

The very first crustaceans rose into being deep in the ocean some half-billion years ago. They drew upon the abundant calcium in seawater, building it into their hard, segmented shells. In time, the progeny of those early crustaceans came to press for the biologic frontier, evolving a little, looking for open niches into which they could swim, adapt, prosper. Eventually, some reached the great divide between ocean and freshwater. The latter was markedly riskier habitat, being calcium-lean and prone to extremes of heat and cold, flood and drought. And it contained competition: aquatic insects. But some crustaceans pressed on into freshwater despite the hazards. And some prevailed.

One of the staunchest survivors in this new territory has been the crayfish. There are some 26,000 species in the class Crustacea, and five hundred of them are crayfish. They established themselves on every continent save Antarctica (they were introduced into Africa in the 1960s) and they range in size from the inch-long dwarf crayfish to a sixteen-inch, eight-pound Tasmanian species. In North America alone, some 350 species occur, inhabiting everything from the rockiest mountain streams to the murkiest low-country swamps. Some crayfish thrive on land, burrowing down to graze the water table with huge, spatulate claws that are modified for little more than shoveling soil. Others spend their sightless lives on the floor of subterranean caves, squeezing oxygen from the humid air.

In watery places like Louisiana, crayfish are abundant. The state boasts 35 species of them, two of which—the red and the white—grow big enough to excite the Cajun palate. To the dismay of some, states like Florida, Alabama, and even Tennessee have more species of crayfish than does Louisiana. With 66 species, Georgia has almost twice as many. But only Louisiana has anything like a true crayfish industry, the annual yield there being on the order of 40 million pounds. California and Oregon—where red crayfish have been introduced—produce about a million pounds a year. With an aggregate annual production of about 50,000 pounds, the Great Lakes area is the last crayfish producer worth mention.

While man may be the most conspicuous predator of crayfish in the Atchafalaya Basin—commercial, sport, and table fishermen together may take as many as 65 million pounds in a really good year—he is by no means the only one. Raccoons, mink, birds, fish, snakes, turtles, and virtually every other creature that coexists in crayfish habitat eat crayfish at one time or another. Sometimes when you pick up a bullfrog, he'll crunch, he's so full of crayfish. It's only fair that everything should eat crayfish, because crayfish will eat almost anything. Unique among crustaceans, crayfish are polytrophic. That means they'll feed anywhere on the food chain. Mostly, they eat detritus, but they also eat plants directly, and even small animals—worms, mollusks, insects, and smaller crustaceans like copepods.

When confronted, a crayfish will rear up to brandish its claws and will back off with short, powerful jerks of the abdomen and tail fan. This puts distance—and raises a curtain of silt—between prey and predator. If the aggressor should latch onto a crayfish leg, the victim can by muscular reflex snap it off at the narrowest point. This small break will clot quickly, and in time the limb will grow back, but if wounded elsewhere crustaceans bleed to death rather easily.

Unable to float, and only poor swimmers at best, crayfish are bottom-dwellers. But they can feed at the surface. By violently flipping its tail, a crayfish can propel itself in an arc to the surface, where it can pick off floating food before sinking to the bottom.

SHAD:
POOR MAN'S SALMON

TEXT BY EDWARD R. RICCIUTI · PHOTOGRAPHY BY CAROLE ALLEN

For years, during these heady weeks of May, the commercial shad fishermen of the lower Connecticut River have worked their reaches by night, often staying out until light edges into the sky above the hills behind the eastern shore. Each reach, a stretch of river bounded by unwritten agreement, has its own complement of fishermen, who have staked claim to it by repeated, sometimes inherited, use.

Night after night, tough, tired men in small boats let out gill nets, drift the reach with the tide, then haul, expectantly watching the dark water for the silvery flash that means enmeshed shad.

A bigger, feistier cousin of the herring, the American shad *(Alosa sapidissima)* is beloved by gourmets for its delicate flesh and tangy roe, and esteemed by anglers for its fight, which has earned it the sobriquet "the poor man's salmon." Selling their catch locally or to the Fulton Fish Market in New York City, the gill-netters who fish the thirty-odd miles of river between Rocky Hill, south of Hartford, and Long Island Sound can earn up to a few thousand dollars each in perhaps six weeks of grueling work.

Like salmon, shad are anadromous, re-turning from the sea to spawn in the same rivers where they were hatched. Shad occur from the Gulf of St. Lawrence in Canada to Florida's St. Johns River, as well as on the West Coast, to which they were transplanted in the 1870s. Deep-bodied and silver-sided, shad spawn as early as January in the southern portion of their range, while the run in the Connecticut, which reputedly produces the best-tasting fish, begins fitfully in April and winds down by early June.

As many as 900,000 fish may pass upriver during a run, drawing anglers in droves as well as commercial netters. River towns celebrate the arrival of the shad with fishing derbies and bakes; tacked on planks, the catch sizzles to a golden brown before open fires. The shad run is a tradition, a ritual of spring.

The tradition, however, has a dimension beyond commerce, sport, and good times. The shad run speaks of the river's resilience and capacity to support life in wondrous abundance if given the chance, a reminder of a bountiful past and a hint of future potential.

During the colonial era shad ran all the way upstream to Bellows Falls, Vermont, 173 miles from the river's mouth and a short piece north of the Massachusetts border. If one can believe reports from those days, the river was clogged with millions of shad when the run was at its peak. Starting a few years after the American Revolution, however, the river was dammed at various upstream falls and rapids, cutting off the spawning grounds north of Turners Falls, Massachusetts. By the middle of the last century, shad could travel no farther north than the dam at Holyoke, about half the original migratory distance upstream. The loss of spawning grounds, together with pollution and heavy fishing pressure, reduced the Connecticut run to a mere thousands of fish, and the situation was as bad if not worse in other rivers.

An alarmed federal government and the various states took steps to conserve the shad, largely by stocking eggs and fry and restricting fishing. With this sort of help, despite occasional relapses, the shad recovered, so that by the late 1800s the runs in the Connecticut and some other rivers were again respectable, even if not as immense as in bygone times.

Quite likely, moreover, the Connecticut run will increase in years to come. Power companies that operate dams across the Connecticut have built fishways over them, opening upstream spawning grounds that have been closed since before the Civil War.

Shad spawn in broad, shallow pools where the current is moderate. On the average, female shad lay more than 200,000 eggs each. After a half-dozen days, the young shad hatches. It lives off its yolk sac for a short while, then feeds on minuscule crustaceans, adding progressively larger insects as it grows. Unlike adult shad, which eat mostly plankton, the young have teeth that are lost at maturity.

By autumn, the shad of the year are fingerlength and heading downriver to the sea, where they remain for four or five years as they grow to adult size—usually three or four pounds but rarely more than twice that. At sea, shad are migratory. They summer north of Cape Cod in the Gulf of Maine, moving south as the water cools in autumn. Exactly where they go is something of a mystery, but apparently it is off the Middle Atlantic or southeastern coast. Shad tagged off Maine, for instance, have turned up as far south as North Carolina.

Spring sends the Connecticut River shad north with those from other streams in the Northeast. Following the warming waters, the fish work their way up the Middle Atlantic Coast, the breeders peeling off into their native streams as they go. Especially in the southern part of their range, few shad survive spawning, although some from the Connect-

icut return the next year, and even a year or two after that.

During April, the Connecticut River shad concentrate in Long Island Sound near the stream's mouth, waiting for the river to warm to temperatures in the neighborhood of 50 degrees Fahrenheit. A strong spring freshet of cold water will delay their entry into the river, but sooner or later they start upstream.

Since midwinter, meanwhile, the commercial fishermen have been repairing their nets, usually more than a thousand feet long and twenty feet deep, with a diamond-shaped mesh of slightly more than five inches. Once the shad enter the river in force the gill-netters fish every night but Friday and Saturday, which are closed to fishing as a conservation measure. They work by night because the nets are much less visible to the shad than during the day.

Henry Golet and Bob Blaschik, who hail from the river towns of Old Lyme and East Haddam, respectively, crew one of the two-man boats. They are linemen for Northeast Utilities, the power company that operates the dams at Holyoke and, farther north, Turners Falls, Massachusetts. Linemen are well paid, but every year Golet and Blaschik take time off to net shad. "It's a tradition," explains Golet, whose father was a shad-netter and riverman before him.

Linemen tend to be rugged customers, and Golet and Blaschik fit the image. Golet is lean and stringy, Blaschik is broad and chunky, and both have the look of men who have spent much of their time outdoors. They fish the Dunn Reach, so called because it stretches between the old Dunn House on the river's west bank and the East Haddam bridge, about two miles south.

Each spring on the Connecticut River, gill-netters work their reaches from dusk to dawn in pursuit of spawning shad, prized by gourmets for their delicate flesh and tangy roe.

This night they will drift downstream, so they tie up at dusk to a pier not far from the Dunn House to wait for dark. They are first on the reach, which by custom means they will have the initial drift, often the most productive. People talk about violence between shad fishermen when someone breaks the traditional rules of the reach. Golet scoffs at these stories, but he admits he would not look kindly on anyone who did break with tradition.

While they wait the fishermen arrange their gear in their sixteen-foot skiff, the deck of which is coated with large, thick, shiny scales. Although heavy and hard, the scales of shad detach easily. Other skiffs and scows are shooting upriver, and greetings echo over the water as they pass. The men of the shad boats, like the watermen of the Chesapeake and the catfish-netters of the Tennessee River, form a local subculture, a link with simpler, more individualistic times before con-

dominiums appeared in the river hamlets.

With darkness, the lights of the East Haddam bridge wink on. Water and shore merge into a black void. The rich smell of marshes and mud rides the breeze. While Blaschik maneuvers the skiff with oars, Golet stands near the bow and lets out the net. Yard after yard disappears into the murky water, buoyed by oval cork floats every six feet along the top and stretched taut by ring-shaped weights at opposite points below. Putting out the net properly calls for experience, an understanding of the river's currents and snags, and wordless cooperation between oarsman and netter. When laid properly, the net stretches out in a relatively straight line perpendicular to the shore, with brightly gleaming lamps riding on donut-shaped floats marking each end.

After three-quarters of an hour, the drift ends. Blaschik rows slowly upstream while his partner hauls the net aboard. It is not ex-

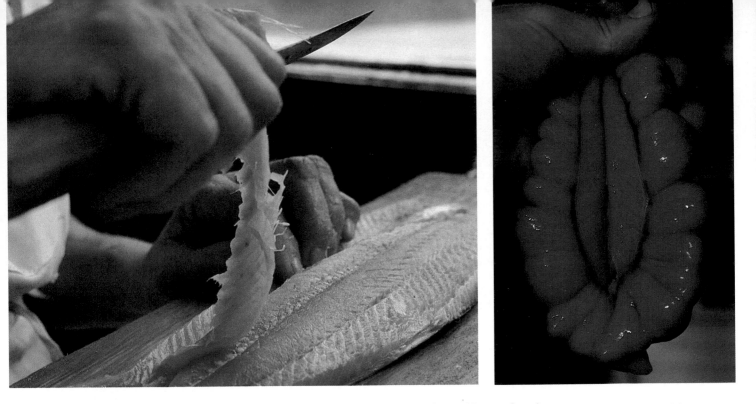

Shad boning is a delicate and dying art. Shad roe is an eating delicacy.

actly bursting with fish. As Golet brings it in hand over hand, the shad come up individually, several yards apart. He holds the slippery body of each fish between his legs while he extracts it from the mesh, then tosses it flopping to the deck. By the time all the net is in the boat, the catch numbers a couple of dozen fish.

Some, often thrown back, are "racers," fish that have already spawned and are returning to the sea exhausted and emaciated. Their flesh is translucent and mushy, second-rate compared with shad that have not yet spawned. Most prized are the full-bodied females, or roes, carrying masses of unfertilized eggs in bulging ovaries. Like caviar, the roe of the sturgeon, shad roe is a delicacy to people who savor such things. The slimmer males, or bucks, also are marketable for their flesh alone, although they bring about a quarter a pound while the roes are sold to markets at more than twice that.

Much of the shad caught by the rivermen goes on retail sale at the local fish markets, some open only during the season. One, in the town of Haddam, is Spencer's Shad Shack, a small wooden building not far from the Dunn Reach. Spencer's closes at the end of this month, when most of the shad caught in the nearby river are racers.

Fishermen bring their catch to Spencer's Shack by 4:00 A.M. Workers who have arrived in the wee hours remove the roe and clean the fish before turning them over to the two or three boners, who sit at newspaper-covered tables in the front room. Shad-boning techniques perfected earlier in the century gave the fishery a great shot in the

arm because they made cooking and eating the flesh much more practical. The shad is a very tricky fish to eat unless its 1,500 bones are removed.

Irene Larsen is one of Spencer's boners. During the season she rises daily at 3:00 A.M. for the hour's drive to Haddam from her home in Willimantic, a city east of the river. Boning shad is a folk art she learned many years ago, not from locals who jealously guarded their techniques but from a man at the Fulton Fish Market in Manhattan whom she paid for the lesson. Some local boners are still secretive about the process, but Larsen is eager to teach novices because there are not enough skilled boners to go around.

Larsen works with several razor-sharp knives, changing the table's covering of newspaper frequently. The boning process is terrifically complex and takes a deft and practiced hand. It is hard for the eye to follow the quick movements of Larsen's fingers as she maneuvers and folds strips of flesh and bones with one hand while working the knife artfully with the other. She finishes a fish in two or three minutes, places the fillets on a stack, and then begins another shad.

Even as Larsen works, over in the river the shad continue to swim upstream. They are invisible for the most part, but every so often a brief streak of silver in the muddy water, like a meteor in the night sky, signals that one has passed by. North of Hartford the river becomes shallower and narrower. Here is where most sport fishing for shad is carried on. Some fishermen try deep holes in the lower few miles of the Farmington River, near its confluence with the Connecticut.

105

Others line up on an old bridge that spans the stream between Windsor Locks on the west and East Windsor across the way.

A few miles north of the bridge, between Suffield on the west and Enfield on the east, lies the Enfield Dam, by tradition the country's best spot for shad angling. The dam is an ancient timber structure, some six feet high, which has been patched over the years with boilerplate and concrete. It was built so that water could be diverted into a canal around its western end, allowing boats to circumvent a series of dangerous rapids. The low dam was not a complete barrier, but passageways were limited, so the shad—delayed in their upstream movement—pooled below it in immense numbers. No place else were the chances of hooking into a shad so good. Fishermen jamming the bank on both sides of the river seemed as thick as the shad in the water. Often, there was bedlam as cheek-by-jowl anglers flailed away with spinning and fly rods, crossing lines, hooking one another, often pushing and shoving, arguing, and sometimes fighting.

Although Enfield Dam still draws a crowd, the fishermen are fewer because the shad congregations are smaller. No longer maintained, the dam has been breached in several places. The number of shad concentrating below the dam is less than half that of a few years past and probably will decrease as the structure continues to deteriorate.

Shad angling really began on the Connecticut River a half-century ago when fishermen—at first accidentally, the story goes—found that these fish would hit shiny lures. Being plankton feeders, shad would not logically seem to be the type of fish to go after lures; besides, during their spawning journeys they do not feed, period. For unknown reasons, however, they snap up certain lures, perhaps because they are in a high state of excitement and irritable, or else because they are territorial at this time.

The standard lures are shad darts, cone-shaped bits of lead weighing less than an ounce, painted bright colors, and tufted with bucktail or nylon bristles. But certain flies, spinners, spoons, and other lures also attract shad. Ask most fishermen who have grown up around the Enfield Dam, however, and they will suggest colorful beads strung above a bare, gold-plated hook.

With the Enfield Dam breached, the best shad angling on the river now is a short distance north below the huge dam at Holyoke, where the Northeast Utilities subsidiary that operates it, Holyoke Water Power Company, holds a fishing derby in early June, when the greatest numbers of fish arrive. In season, the rocky, rapid waters below the Holyoke Dam seem alive with shad. They battle the surging current, knifing through the turbulent water, but to no avail. The journey ends on the broad apron of the dam, a smooth expanse of concrete slanted downstream and covered with a thin sheet of whitewater. Wriggling and finning, sometimes leaping, the shad struggle to inch their way up the apron, their backs arched and exposed above the water. Their progress blocked by the towering face of the dam, the shad tire and one by one are swept back with the current. Their journey does not end, however, despite the presence of the dam.

Since 1955, about two million shad have made it past the dam at Holyoke. In that year a fishway was built there, the first successful one for shad on the East Coast. During its first years of operation only a few thousand shad were carried over the dam, but since improvements almost a decade ago, the number has surpassed 300,000 annually.

The fishway consists of two lifts, square metal hoppers that are in effect elevators for fish. They rest at the foot of the dam where currents eventually will draw the shad—which align themselves against the downstream flow of water—into them. When enough fish enter the channel leading to a lift, an operator near the top of the dam activates a movable gate that closes behind the fish and moves forward on tracks, herding them into the hopper. Jammed with shiny, flopping fish—blueback herring and lamprey as well as shad—the hopper rises fifty-two feet to a flume, where they are dumped. It leads over the dam to the river.

As they swim against the current through the 300-foot-long flume, the fish pass a port where biologists from the river states can observe and count them. Some shad are removed with a fish trap for transplantation to other rivers in nearby northeastern states to help restore lost shad runs.

Shad, however, are no longer the only interest of biologists who man the fish trap and viewing station. They are more excited about Atlantic salmon, which were driven from the river by the same pressures that diminished the shad. The river states and the federal government are attempting to restore the salmon by releasing young in the stream in hopes they will return to spawn as adults,

now that much of the river is freer of pollution than for many years past. Some salmon
have come back, stealing the limelight because they are sexier gamefish.

The commercial shad fishery alone has a
$500,000 annual retail value, while the
chances that the river will again support even
a modest salmon run are still iffy. Be that as it
may, the prospects of salmon in the river once
more have added impetus to the building of
fishways above Holyoke. Northeast Utilities
opened a $13-million network of three fish
ladders over the dam at Turners Falls three
years ago. It seems to work for salmon, but
the shad have not negotiated it with any real
success.

Lyle Thorpe, a woodsy yet scholarly biologist, thinks he knows why. Fresh out of Cor-
nell University in 1935, Thorpe was the first
biologist hired by the Connecticut State
Board of Fisheries and Game. Retiring as director of fish and game for the state in 1964,
he went to work as a fisheries consultant to
Northeast Utilities and has been a devil's ad-
vocate on environmental matters for the
company ever since.

There is way too much turbulence in the
fish ladders for the shad which, although
they take rough water, cannot handle it as
well as salmon, suggests Thorpe. In 1982 he
conceived a modification to one of the fish
ladders, blocking off some of the orifices
through which water flows to reduce the turbulence. The company made the changes,
and as things turned out, between 13,000
and 14,000 of the shad from the multitudes
below Turners Falls have climbed the ladder.

After clearing the falls, the next dam is at
Vernon, Vermont, 142 miles from the river's
mouth. A $10-million fishway was installed
there in June 1981 by the New England
Power Company, a generating subsidiary of
the New England Electric System.

A few thousand shad that managed to as-
cend the Turners Falls fishways have climbed
the Vernon fishway. So, once over the Turners
Falls fish ladders, the run should continue on
past Vernon. From there the sailing is clear
up to Bellows Falls, historically the northern-
most limit of the Connecticut shad run. If that
happens, then the Connecticut River shad,
for the first time in almost 200 years, will
have reclaimed all of their ancestral waters.

V

WILD PLANTS AND MAN

TREES THAT WEEP, WHISTLE, AND GROW KITTENS

BY JOHN MADSON

There's a certain small song that seems to stay with me—I can't recall where it came from, but it faithfully expresses one of my basic attitudes:

"Oh, I wish I was a willow on the riverbank
'Cause I'd never have to make a living then.
Just look up the river, and down the river,
Then up the river again . . . "

That's about all I remember. Still, it shows what some of us have in common with willows—not just a singular lack of ambition, but an attraction to such appealing places as the banks of bright little trout streams, the sandbars of slow brown catfish rivers, and marsh edges and alpine meadows.

Willows have a way of inhabiting some very good places, growing as trees or shrubs from beach dunes at sea level to the upper tree line of our highest mountains, from desert arroyos to Arctic barrens. They go by many names. Some are named for a physical feature: the crack willow, peachleaf, red, black, white, shining, heart-leaved, weeping, littletree, felt-leaf, yew-leaf, balsam, satiny, and pussy willows. Others wear place names: sandbar, arroyo, river, meadow, Northwest, Florida, Missouri, Pacific, Sitka. There are willows named for their describers: Bebb, Tracy, Gooding, Hooker, Scouler, Bonpland, and Hinds.

It's not clear how many distinct species of willows exist in North America. No tree family appears to be tougher to systematize; willows can be a field naturalist's nightmare and a plant taxonomist's dream, for they have a maddening tendency to hybridize. One authority cites "over a hundred species." Another puts the total at "more than sixty-five species." Still another just notes that "from eighty to a hundred species" are distributed from the Gulf to the Arctic Circle. Swedish botanist Eric Hulten lists over fifty distinct species of willows for Alaska and its neighboring territories alone. There's not even a consensus on how many willows are actually trees. Fewer than half our North American willows ever reach tree size; most range from large shrubs to low, sprawling mats, and one botanist notes that only about twenty-five species of willows ever attain tree size. Another puts the number at about thirty-four, while that estimable naturalist-writer Donald Culross Peattie sensibly straddled the issue by noting that "all the tree species are also frequently shrubby, while many of the habitually shrubby species are sometimes twenty to twenty-five feet tall." Anyway, there are at least eighty species of North American willows, sharing membership in the family Salicaceae with ten species of poplars. All in all a northerly family, and nearly all our willows, poplars, aspens, and cottonwoods are in temperate or north temperate climes.

The willow genus *Salix* is derived from the Celtic *sal,* meaning "near," and *lis,* meaning "water." Almost without exception, willows are inordinately fond of water—ask any householder who has planted a willow over a sewer line. Here in our corner of the world along the Upper Mississippi, they are the trees closest to the river, crowding down past the low banks and growing in great profusion out there on the mudflats and sandbars.

The Mississippi is a river of willows. From its source all the way down its main stem to its mouth, the river's banks, islands, and low flats are clad with willows. When new sandbars are thrown up by floodwaters or Corps of Engineers' channel dredging, or mudflats are revealed during prolonged low water, some of the first plants to pioneer these raw, naked places are willows. They come on in dense knee-high stands, sometimes as many as 10,000 seedlings on a half-acre of mudflat. Just behind them, on somewhat higher

Above: Pussy willow (Salix discolor), *Maine, by Dwight R. Kuhn. Previous page: Pacific willow* (Salix lasiandra), *Idaho, by Joanne Pavia.*

111

Below: Lindheimer black willow (Salix nigra lindheimeri), *Texas, by Wyman P. Meinzer.*

ground may be older stands of larger willows—venerable trees nearing the end of their forty-year life span—backed, in turn, by towering cottonwoods or silver maples.

Willows are finely tuned to life along the water. Their sexual cycle begins in early spring, and the seeds ripen at about the time rivers and creeks are bank-full. The mature willow catkins emit clouds of light, silken fluff. Each bit of fluff carries a tiny seed and is light enough to be airborne but not so light that it flies for great distances. If the airborne seed only manages a few yards between the tree and the nearest water it will have followed its flight plan and its manifest destiny, for some willows are more readily distributed by water than any other means. At least this is true of such riverine species as the peachleaf, Missouri, and sandbar willows. A willow embryo has a very thin covering and can germinate within a few hours but only if it finds a moist seed bed. Otherwise, it loses viability within two or three days. Seeds falling on dry ground, especially on dry, shaded ground under old trees, have hardly a chance.

River willows seed at a prodigious rate; there are times in spring when calm Mississippi sloughs appear to have been sprayed with silvery flocking, when the edges of sandbars and mudbanks are whitish mats of new willow seeds, and some of the channel catfish taken in our basket traps have bellies full of the stuff. But even if most of the seeds strewn so lavishly along a mudflat manage to germinate and produce a dog-hair stand of sprouts, and even if most of these survive further immersion by more high water, the process of natural culling is in play from the very beginning. Most will perish as the stand grows older and some saplings begin to overtop others, for shade is deadly to willows. Floods they can take—and burning sun and the abrasion of blowing sand, and hunters cutting them by countless boatloads for brushing duck blinds—but shade is intolerable.

Willows are a notable part of any fine Mississippi River day—and are just as notable on a summer night.

There are special smells to night water and wet sand that go with tending trotlines from an island camp. There's the clean, fresh smell of the catfish taken off the lines under the summer stars, and the blessed coolness that has pooled under the limerock ledges of places like Infidel Hollow and then flowed down the creekways into the main river valley with the breath of ferns and wet stone and hidden spring seeps that have never known the sun. And there is the night breath of

willows—a subtle pungency from the tiny resin glands of millions of leaves warmed by the summer sun and now cooling at night. In her fine book *River World,* Virginia Eifert remarked on this "perfume of the Mississippi." She noticed it most strongly one night on the lower river when she was a passenger on a towboat: "To me, the first time I smelled it, it was a haunting, honeysuckle-like fragrance. I asked what it was. 'That's the willow smell,' said the captain, almost reverently."

Most of these river willows are the ubiquitous sandbar willows, pioneers of the mudflats and new sandbars, first of the trees to establish beachheads on new ground. They never grow to much more than twenty feet, with spindly trunks only a few inches thick, but in addition to thickly seeding a barren sandbar these willows can also send out undergrown stems to form dense thickets or "willow bats." (I've never been able to learn the origin of that term. But there's no doubting the origin of "willow slaps," which means the same thing. Just walk closely behind someone through a dense stand of willows and find out.)

Another major Mississippi River willow is the black willow, largest of all American willows. Here along our Upper Mississippi we rarely see one much over fifty feet tall, but far downriver in the rich bottoms of the

Lower Mississippi it is a giant of a willow that may be 140 feet high with a trunk nearly four feet in diameter. It's also one of the few willows with any commercial lumber value. Not that it rates very highly. The wood is soft, light, and not very strong. Still, it has uses. It isn't easily split by nails, and its springy fibers tend to grip nails better than most woods. Black willow lumber is very durable in water and has the unusual ability to sustain bad dents and bruises without splintering. Just the thing for waterwheels and certain boat keels. But one of its greatest values—and one shared by most of the river willows—is a masterful capacity for tying down easily eroded riverbanks.

Willows are professional erosion-controllers. It is their business to lock riparian soils in place; they and their ecological niches depend entirely on their success in doing so. They accomplish this by rapid growth, swift development of the matted, densely tangled root systems, spreading by underground stolons, and the ability of odd bits of broken green parts to take root and sprout. For protecting streambanks from severe cutting, willows can be more serviceable and practical than masonry walls or shields of the heavy rock facing called riprap. One of the many enigmas of modern agribusiness is why some landowners permit streams to gnaw at their richest fields when the problem might be

solved with a bit of bulldozer work and some green willow sticks.

If a stream's banks are vertical and caving, it is probably necessary to do some grading (during low-water periods) to create gradual slopes that can be planted with willow cuttings. These can range from green wands cut from year-old shoots to green stakes several inches in diameter. Stick them into the soft ground with the larger stakes down toward the water's edge and they will all grow vigorously. On the bends of small streams whose banks already have some natural slope, willow stakes up to four inches in diameter can be driven rather closely together from the water's edge on up the bank. The spaces between these green stakes can be filled with green cuttings from willow trees. Such cuttings should touch the ground as much as possible; even better, they can be lightly buried. Any part of a live willow will grow vigorously if placed in moist soil.

On a steep, caving bank where grading may not be practical, another tack can be taken. Willow poles about twenty feet long are cut in spring before growth begins and laid on the ground near the streambank several feet apart, butts toward the stream. Woven wire fencing is fastened to the poles, with two feet of each pole projecting below the wire if the stream edge is soft mud, and less for a firm bank. With wire fastened to the poles—in sections about a hundred feet long—the whole thing is pushed over so that the butts of the poles sink into the soft mud at the water's edge. As the banks cave away, some of the soil will lodge on the wire and partly bury the poles, which take root and grow.

Primeval belts of floodplain timber that flanked the old Mississippi prevented the sort of terrible erosion that began with settlement. But as the riparian forests were cleared for farm fields and cut for steamboat fuel, the unprotected banks were devoured by the ravenous river—especially on the outer swings of bends where the current was most violent.

Enter a young captain of the Army Corps of Engineers, Oswald Ernst, who reported to the St. Louis district office in 1878 and proceeded to enlist willows in his personal war against riverbank erosion. Ernst pioneered the use of huge willow "mattresses" as part of bank revetments along the Mississippi. At a problem area he would first divide the eroding bank into three zones: from the lowest point of erosion up to the low-water mark, from there up to the level where willows would grow, and from the "willow zone" up to the top of the riverbank.

Overleaf: Black willow (Salix nigra), *Minnesota, by Jim Brandenburg.*

113

Missouri willow (Salix eriocephala), *Minnesota, by R. Hamilton Smith.*

The commonest willows at hand (peach-leaf, sandbar, and black) were woven into huge mats that were usually about 1,000 feet long, 250 feet wide, and a foot thick. These were pulled out into the river and sunk under a ballast of heavy rock with the upper portions of the mattress at about the low-water mark. Above that mark the bank was graded to a 1:3 slope and paved with heavy rock; willow mattresses were not used because that zone would be alternately above and below water and a mattress would quickly rot. (A constantly submerged mattress might last thirty years.) From the rip-rapped zone of rock to the top of the bank, Ernst planted willows—an indigenous river tree that he had studied intensively, just as any good engineer studies the structural components of his profession.

At about the same time, settlers in the central prairie states were finding that willows were the answer to a sodbuster's prayer for a faster-growing, hardy windbreak. Better hardwoods and conifers would follow, of course, but there was no beating willow (especially crack willow) as a nurse tree: It was easily planted, fairly long-lived, needed little care, had some fuel value, and was able to reproduce vigorously from the stump.

In those earliest days of the frontier, however, certain drawbacks to willows had been noted. In 1833 Prince Maximilian von Wied Neuwied was at Fort Osage on the Missouri River, where he collected the Missouri willow and was the first to describe it. He also reflected in his notes: "The driftwood on the sandbank, consisting of the trunks of large timber trees, forms a scene characteristic of the North American rivers; at least I saw nothing like it in Brazil, where most of the rivers rise in the primeval mountains, or flow through more solid ground. On the banks which we now passed, the drifted trunks of trees were in many places already covered with sand; a border of willows and poplars was before the forest, and it is among these willow bushes that the Indians usually lie in ambush, when they intend to attack those who tow their vessels up the river by long ropes."

Willows are often assigned the gloomier corners of folklore and literature.

Take, for example, the chilling short story "The Willows" by Algernon Blackwood, one of England's masters of the supernatural genre. Two young canoeists are on holiday on the Danube. In near-flood conditions, they make camp on a willow-grown island and soon learn that the island is one of those

116

dread places where "the veil is thin" and forces in the Fourth Dimension can probe blindly into our world. They are "found" when the canoe is probed and destroyed—and then the terrible groping proceeds to follow them through the willows, leaving pits like giant ant-lion traps. Just the sort of story needed at a float trip campfire.

Then there's the malevolent Old Man Willow in J. R. R. Tolkien's *Lord of the Rings.* This was "a huge willow tree, old and hoary. Enormous it looked, its sprawling branches going up like reaching arms with many long-fingered hands, its knotted and twisted trunk gaping in wide fissures that creaked faintly as the boughs moved." Old Man Willow had a propensity for lulling travelers to sleep under his branches, and then splitting open his trunk and slowly engulfing them.

On the other hand, there's Kenneth Grahame's graceful little classic *The Wind in the Willows,* which deals most kindly with conservative water rats, moles, and badgers, flamboyant toads, and the genus *Salix.* It's an appealing premise, for I've always regarded willows as congenial associates in myriad fine, small adventures.

Such were the Old Man Willows of my Iowa boyhood—several gnarled old trees clinging to the verge of the prairie creek that wandered through a broad pasture on the next farm. They were the only trees in that piece of grassland, and there was nothing in the least malevolent about them, with roots buttressing the black soil of the creekbank and providing the only eddies deep enough for any worthwhile skinny-dipping—and the only real shade along the creek, to boot.

Green-willow days. With the first real blush of spring, at about the time shadblow was blooming, we'd stop playing "territory" and mumbletypeg long enough to cut lengths of willow as thick as our thumbs and six inches long. A couple of inches from one end, a ring was cut through the bark. At about the same distance from the other end, a deep notch. Then, with that all-purpose, wholly indispensable jackknife, you would tap the green bark of this willow piece until it began to loosen and could be pulled off as an intact cylinder. The bare wood of the notched end would be whittled to form an air passage and air chamber. The tube of bark would be slipped back into place, notch properly aligned over the air chamber, and the tranquillity of a soft spring day would be rent with piercing shrills.

Then summer came on—the season reigned over by his freckle-flanked majesty, King Catfish—and there was nothing handier for carrying home a mess of fresh-caught "fiddlers" than a limber switch of sandbar willow run through mouths and gills and then knotted at the tip.

Even in winter there were uses for willows. Somewhere—probably in *Deep-River Jim's Trail Book*—I read that it was possible to make emergency snowshoes from the easily bent willow branches. This was eventually accomplished with several sandbar willows and lengths of binder twine. I never did get the harness right and was unable to stride over the drifts as old Deep-River said I could, but the outfit worked after a fashion. In the process, though, we learned another good thing about willows—that certain dense willow slaps within the bends of our home river could be expected to feed and shelter substantial numbers of cottontail rabbits during the harshest winter weather. In years to come, we would learn that the same thing applied to Alaskan moose and willow ptarmigan.

No doubt about it. Willows were useful for lots of things, not all of which were necessarily good. Pity the kid with a weeping willow in the yard and a mother who yelled: "I've had all the sass from you I can put up with! You go out and cut a good strong willer switch *and bring it in here to me!*" (Dr. Spock, where were you when we needed you?)

Of course, Indians knew how to use willows in many ways, and not just for ambushes along the Big Muddy. The sweat baths of the plains tribes, those ritual saunas so important in certain purification rites, were often small domes of bent willow poles and branches covered with buffalo hides or blankets. Sweat baths completed, the warriors might confer while smoking kinnikinnick, an aromatic mixture whose formula varied with different Indian nations but often contained the dried inner bark of dogwood or red willow. The bark would be shaved from twigs, spread out to dry, and then finely crushed with hands greased with buffalo fat which would leave just enough grease adhering to the flakes to make them burn well. Too bitter to be smoked alone, willow bark was usually mixed with a bit of Arikara twist tobacco, and some fragrant roots or herbs. Then, as likely as not, this would be smoked by a senior warrior as he took his ease against a handsome backrest of slender willow rods sewn together, while outside the entrance flap of the lodge hung his buffalo-hide war shield with a frame of bent willow.

Nowhere are willows more prevalent than in the Far North, and the Ojibway and other northern people use willow to smoke-cure some of their leathers. From my study wall

Overleaf: Weeping willow (Salix babylonica), *Holland, by Kees Van Den Berg (Photo Researchers).*

117

hangs a pair of knee-high moosehide winter moccasins, handsomely trimmed with bear fur and bands of appliqué with colored woolen tassels hanging down the sides, and the soft leather still carries the sweet incense of the willow smoke with which it was cured.

Those moccasins came from beyond the upper end of Lake Athabaska in country that is increasingly given over to willows until, as one comes out into the great barrens, there is nothing that can really be called a tree. The stunted firs and spruces of the *tit-chin-nichile* or "land of little sticks" begin giving out, surrendering to muskeg and the scrub willows that are eventually reduced to sprawling mats only a few inches high.

A stand of scrub willow in the Far North can be terrible stuff to walk through—a dense, thigh-deep fastness of tough stems and branches too high to step over and too low to bull your way through as you might in a stand of taller willows. To make it worse, such willows are often the vegetative pioneers that overlie glacial rubble and old rockslides, and under the tangle of branches is the sort of footing that breaks bones. Still, nothing is all bad. As firewood, the dead, bleached willow stems and twigs of the tundra are far better than the next best thing, which is no fuel at all. One of the finest meals we've ever eaten, after an unbroken diet of dehydrated food, was of savory caribou cutlets broiled to a turn over a little fire of willow twigs in the Alaskan barrens.

Certain low, dense configurations of willows also occur in the High West and can be just as maddening. O frustration, thy name is Bebb willow as it grows along the banks of little cutthroat trout runs in the High Country! By arching entirely over those little brooks, or crowding in closely enough to block any real flycasting, or by conspiring with tag alders around certain beaver ponds, willows can be some of the best friends a trout has.

Of all the willows of North America the best known to the public at large (and usually the *only* ones known) are the weeping willow and pussy willow.

The weeping willow is native to China, coming to North America via Europe. It's a favored ornamental that gets up to sixty feet high, its long, slender, drooping branches sweeping the ground, inspiring melancholy and such song lyrics as "Willow, weep for me," and "Come all ye young maidens, and Listen to me/Don't hang your hearts on the green willow tree." Sad willow songs go back a long way; the first may have sprung from the grief of the Israelites and out of the harp of King David himself, who sang in the 137th Psalm: "By the rivers of Babylon, there we sat down, yea, we wept, when we remembered Zion. We hanged our harps upon the willows in the midst thereof."

This inspired the great taxonomist Carolus Linnaeus to name the weeping willow *Salix babylonica,* although certain botanical agnostics have challenged this, claiming that the trees of the rivers of Babylon were almost certainly alders or poplars, and most assuredly not weeping willows. Anyway, it was under a weeping willow on St. Helena that Napoleon Bonaparte dreamed in exile of *his* lost Zions. He was buried near that tree, and for many years its cuttings were in demand for transplanting through much of Europe—but, presumably, not in Russia.

The weeping willow was introduced into North America in 1730 and soon became a favored carving for headstones, along with index fingers pointing skyward over the legend "There is rest in Hev'n." When weeping willows fell out of fashion for headstones, they began appearing in lithographs, their drooping branches framing copiously weeping ladies with such captions as "News From The Battlefield."

At least as well known as the weeping willow, but a lot more cheerful, is the pussy willow, *Salix discolor.* This is mainly a tree of the Northeast and Upper Midwest, and in late winter or very early spring the leafless branches suddenly produce ranks of the velvety, silver-gray male catkins that are sure signs of better times ahead even though there are still patches of snow along the northerly hillsides. After a week or two the furry catkins mature and begin producing pollen of the brightest gold. One of my earliest fishing memories is of chubs in the ice-cold prairie rivers of March with the first of the wild honeybees working at clumps of pussy willow. The land belonged to winter as much as spring, but the bees had found the golden dust of the mature staminate catkins and were busily making "bee bread."

Most people never see the willow flowers that succeed the famous immature catkins in a week or two. The pussy willow twigs are usually discarded when they enter what Peattie called "the awkward age in which they have lost the charm of babyhood and not gained the splendor of maturity." It's worth keeping those twigs in water and enduring their floral adolescence to see those gorgeous golden stamens.

By the way, I just remembered another line of that song:

"But I'll never be a willow on the riverbank...."

Maybe not, but I'll keep working on it.

Leaves of Lemmon's willow (Salix lemmonii), *California, by Steve Terrill.*

121

OF MEN AND MORELS

BY PETER CANBY

The spring of 1981 was a season of great anticipation for mushroom hunters in Boyne City, a small lower-peninsula Michigan town that for the past twenty-two years has hosted the National Mushroom Hunting Championships. The 1981 championship was expected to be a showdown between two local heroes. Dana Shaler, thirty-two, a tall, bearded millwright and four-time champion, was scheduled to meet, head to head, his arch rival, Stan Boris, twenty-nine, equally large, a plumber by trade, all-time record holder, and six-time champion.

Boyne City is the self-proclaimed mushroom capital of the world, but the contest it sponsors concerns itself only with the family Morchellaceae, or morel. This should not be surprising. Morels are the most elusive and prized of the edible fungi. They are found over much of the country but flourish in few places the way they do among the rolling hills, hardwood forests, and farms around Boyne City.

Despite this relative abundance, however, Boyne City morels are not easy to find—even if Stan Boris, in his 1970 championship year, claims to have found 915 of them in ninety minutes. Morels are cone-shaped mushrooms with a distinctive wrinkled cap. They range in color from creamy-brown to near-black and blend in uncannily with the tangled-brown leaf mold of the forest floor. Around Boyne City, morels grow for only a brief period in the spring during a time span too movable to locate accurately on a calendar—and perhaps best described in local mushroom vernacular: "when oak leaves are as big as squirrels' ears," or "when bracken fern is still curled up like a fiddlehead." It is a season in which the morel's natural disguise is compounded many times over by the fact that large numbers of spring plants are pushing up through the drab leaf cover of the winter forest floor. Trillium are out, as well as wild lilies, jack-in-the-pulpit, white violets, and many other plants. Bumblebees stumble drunkenly from flower to flower, and tubers and stalks of all kinds are bulging up from the earth.

There are six commonly agreed upon varieties of North American morels, of which only three are likely to be out in any number at the time of the Boyne City contest. The genus *Morchella* is represented by *M. angusticeps,* the black morel, and by *M. esculenta,* the white morel, which is slightly bigger and whiter and comes up a week to ten days after the black. The third is *Verpa bohemica,* which used to be classified as a false morel and which some people find inedible. However, it is considered harmless enough by the Boyne City judges to be counted along with the two *Morchella* species.

Local wisdom has it that morels are found around stands of poplar, or at the bases of dying elm trees. They also are said to grow in apple orchards and in burnt-over forests of all kinds, but these are the most general of rules and, in Boyne City, there are many exceptions. It almost seems safer to observe that morels are so unpredictable that no one without extensive local experience can say where they will grow from year to year. One Michigan mycologist, reflecting on the difficulty of definition of morel habits and classification, told me: "At a certain level it is pure opinion. Discussing morels over a few beers can be as accurate as discussing them when you're fully sober." Little did I know how apt this observation would prove when, in early May of last year, I set out to pay visits to the two champions—Dana Shaler and Stan Boris—to reap the benefits of their respective insights.

Stan Boris, although a native of Boyne City, lives in the nearby town of Petroskey. He carries a business card that reads: *STAN BORIS. MUSHROOM GUIDE. MUSHROOMS FOR SALE BY THE BUSHEL.* Across the top is written, *I BUY LIONEL ELECTRIC TOY TRAINS.* I telephoned Boris and arranged to meet him late one afternoon in Petroskey.

Boris lives in a green-and-white trailer set on the edge of the road on top of a long, sloping field overlooking Lake Michigan. I was already at the Boris trailer with his wife, Gerry, and a five-year-old son, John, when Boris got back from work. He came in the door wearing a blue windbreaker with *PLUMBERS AND PIPEFITTERS LOCAL 639* written in big yellow letters across the back. Boris is big, hulking, bushy-haired and generally unshaven—entirely unlike any mushroom hunter I had ever imagined. He

When oak leaves are as big as squirrels' ears, and bracken fern is still curled up like a fiddlehead, this most elusive and prized of all edible fungi makes its brief annual appearance. (John Shaw photo)

said nothing as he entered but glanced briefly at me out of the corner of his eye, like a whale swimming past an underwater camera, peeled off his jacket, took a tall bottle of Coca-Cola out of the refrigerator, pulled on a candy-striped, short-brimmed cloth hat, turned to me, stared ominously, and pronounced in a loud voice, "Well, I'm ready."

Boris drove me to a young poplar-maple-beech forest not far from his house. "The way I generally get mushrooms," he explained as we drove, "is to get my chainsaw running at the edge of the woods. I put it on the ground while it's still running so that the mushrooms think I'm cutting wood. I sneak up, pick off the lead mushroom, then round up the rest." Boris laughed loudly at his own joke.

We got out of the car and Boris led the way into an area of long ridges several hundred feet high which were covered with an open hardwood forest. He picked up a long staff from the forest floor and strode off confidently. He was wearing a faded black-and-white-checked flannel shirt and jeans. The jeans hung below his large belly, low on his hips. The empty Coke bottle was thrust jauntily into his back pocket. "I walk at a steady three miles an hour," Boris told me. "I try to spot the mushrooms twenty or thirty feet out. You lose them close up. If I don't see any, I keep moving until I do. They often grow close together, so when I spot one I stop and examine the surrounding area. The main thing is that if you want to find any you've got to keep moving."

Boris explained that the black morels were out and growing in low points along the ridges, where the forest floor was damp but not swampy and where there was a lot of green. "It's been a dry spring," he observed. "They're growing in the places where the snow last went out." He stopped and pulled up a small lily-like plant that was around in great numbers. He peeled back the lower stem and told me to take a bite. It tasted like raw onion. "That's wild leek," he told me. Boris sniffed the air skeptically. "See how the air is different around here? You can smell the leeks in the air. If I were a mushroom I'd want to grow here."

Boris soon began to find mushrooms. But, even mindful of his advice, I was having trouble spotting the morels against the forest floor. I couldn't help looking under my feet, and the effort of scrutinizing so many details made me dizzy. After ten or fifteen minutes, I had one morel in my bag—a black, *Morchella angusticeps*—which I had spotted backlit along a ridge above me, glowing in a shaft of late-afternoon sunlight like a jack-o'-

lantern. Boris looked at my one mushroom, rattled his several dozen, and asked, "Are you going to pick or just stand around watching?" We were near the top of one of the ridges. Boris leaned down and picked a black morel beside a poplar root about a foot away from my right shoe. He dropped it condescendingly in my bag. "That one would have tripped you if I hadn't gotten it." I looked down and noticed a mushroom behind the spot where Boris was standing. I picked it up and dropped it in his bag. He frowned. "There're two things I want to impress on you," he said. "The first is always hire a guide—and I'm the only one I know. The second is never, never, never find a mushroom behind your guide."

A few hours later we returned to Stan Boris' trailer with a few hundred morels—mostly blacks—and a few *Verpa bohemica*, which Boris and other Boyne City residents call "caps," because their caps hang away from their stems like half-furled umbrellas. Boris sat me down with his young son John at one end of the kitchen table while he ate his dinner of fried bologna and boiled potatoes at the other. Under his watchful eye John and I were to clean the mushrooms. We carefully separated the *Verpa bohemica*, which Boris' family would eat, from the marketable *Morchella*. Young John asked me if I wanted to hear a new record of his. He ran into the next room and put it on. It was "Whistle While You Work." We split and washed the mushrooms. Stan's wife, Gerry, sautéed some of the *Morchella* in butter, and I sat and ate a mound of fresh, wild morels while a chorus of Disney woodland creatures whistled cheerfully in the background.

I met Dana Shaler the next day—the evening before the first round of the mushroom contest. Once again I had preceded my guide to the rendezvous, and when Shaler came in, I was sitting at a corner table in Betty's Good Food Restaurant in Boyne Falls eating a piece of homemade lemon-cream pie and eyeing an Amish family at a table nearby. They were as sharply etched and as still as a Vermeer—the father bearded and rigidly immobile, the eyes of the wife and two children darting about nervously. They sat in severe and strained silence. When Shaler joined me I asked about the family. He told me that since the Amish do not drive, these probably had hired a driver to bring them up from Indiana so they could pick mushrooms. "They pick from daylight to dark," Dana told me. He recounted asking a group of them how they'd done. "Not bad," they had told him. "We had five or six bushels at the end of the day."

Dana Shaler is a solid, well-built man with

a thick beard and a deep tan. As a millwright, he installs compressors, generators, elevators, and conveyors—"anything that moves," as he puts it. But this work is a recent calling, and precision is the connecting thread in his extensive previous work history: machining, tool and die and masonry. Dana Shaler had won the mushroom-hunting contest three of the last four years. In 1980, the fine-tuned Shaler mushroom machine was thrown off by a last-minute wisdom tooth extraction and he finished seventh. But he expressed the hope that this time he would be able to regain his title by using his superior experience and finesse against his younger competition.

Shaler got a cup of coffee to go, and we set out for some state land up behind Boyne Falls. We drove up old logging roads along meandering stream beds, through brilliant green fields, budding hardwood stands, and past wild cherry trees in full bloom. It is one of Shaler's proud boasts that he can spot morels from a car moving at fifteen or twenty miles an hour. "I've got good eyes," he explains modestly. Shaler did himself one better. With the truck radio going and Merle Haggard and Johnny Paycheck singing "I'm going off the deep end," with a cup of hot coffee sloshing in one hand while the other was steering around enormous mounds and deep ruts in the road, he was still able to spot a group of morels around the base of a stand of dead elms near the roadside. We got out to look. The three he had spotted turned into a dozen, then two or three dozen, until we had found seventy or eighty in all. They were white morels, *Morchella esculenta,* which tend to cluster more than the blacks. Shaler took out his metal lunch pail and filled it two-thirds of the way up. He looked delighted. "Before this I'd have said that two hundred would have won the contest tomorrow. It's been dry and too cold at night, but with the whites out I'd say it might be more like three or four hundred."

I asked Shaler what his strategy for the contest was. "I generally run out a mile or so to get away from people at the starting point. Then I start prospecting. The main thing is to cover enough ground. I pick a lot of them on the run."

I asked him if he ever got lost. "I never have," he said, "but it happens. Last year Ed Crozier came running over a ridge, and just over the other side was a black bear. Ed froze. The bear came toward him. Ed ran. He didn't stop until he was clear to Petoskey. He flagged down a car when he reached a road and the driver made him trade all his mushrooms for a ride back to Boyne City." Shaler

paused and then added. "At least that's how Ed tells it."

A spring drive on a muddy Boyne City logging road can yield as many as a dozen pickup trucks an hour, all driven by local people hunting for morels. Fresh morels in northern Michigan bring something like $7 to $9 a pound; dried ones, $50 to $100 a pound. [Prices in 1987 approach $12 and $125, respectively.] Although this is not money to scoff at in a rural town, the morels are hard to find, and the cash does not begin to pay for the time it takes to hunt and clean the mushrooms.

The champion of the Boyne City contest achieves a certain local prestige, but there are many local mushroom hunters too busy hunting on their own to enter the contest. Under whatever circumstances they are hunted, however, the morels around Boyne City seem to have an almost mystical hold on the local populace. It is possible that this is rooted in the mushroom's biological role, since fungi seem to exercise a fascinating contempt for the diurnal regimens of green plants. This role is to break down organic compounds, thus making them reusable in simpler forms. The late mycologist Louis Krieger argued that without this fungal process the soil soon would be exhausted and "the remains of plants and animals... would, in a short time, clutter the Earth to such an extent that there would be no getting about."

Mushrooms are produced by only the most highly evolved fungi. The mushroom plant is the mass of white, lace-like mycelium that occurs in the soil. The mushroom itself is the fruit of this largely subsurface plant. It pops up, under the right conditions, for the purpose of spreading the species.

Mushrooms propagate through the dissemination of spores. The mushroom spores are microscopic and single-celled. They exist in incredible numbers and, windborne, drift far and wide into the atmosphere, where they remain aloft for considerable lengths of time. A large puffball, for instance, might contain a trillion spores. Once these spores are released, they are borne off to mingle with the even-more-numerous yeasts, molds, and lesser fungi, so that they become as all-pervasive in the atmosphere as the biological principle of decay which they represent.

But even in the esoteric and unpredictable world of mushroom behavior, morels are famously difficult. Despite the now generally agreed upon species of morels—*Morchella esculenta, Morchella angusticeps, Verpa bohemica,* and so on—there is still considerable controversy about how many morel species

125

there really are. Europeans, for example, describe up to eighty on the basis of different shapes and colors.

The reason for this disparity is that in order to establish the existence of a species, it has to be crossbred with its own kind under controlled conditions—usually in a laboratory. In 1981, morels had never been grown in a laboratory. For forty years the New York Botanical Garden tried unsuccessfully to grow morels. It maintained a laboratory full of test tubes in which morel spores and mycelium were mixed with organic compounds considered conducive to their growth. The mycelium would grow, but the morels would not fruit.

Morels grow in such a variety of conditions, and in such diverse shapes and colors, that what is true for one species of morel in one place may not be true in another. Morels that grow in Boyne City under elms and poplars are found under pines in the Pacific Northwest. Local people know that they are dealing with something elusive, and that—more than money or local fame—enhances their interest in morels. At the mushroom festival there is a souvenir T-shirt that graphically illustrates some of Boyne City's feelings toward the morel. It shows a leprechaun peering out from behind a giant morel, and it bears the caption: "Boyne City, Wild and Free."

The day of the first round of the Boyne City morel championship was overcast and cool. The town's two motels were crowded, and the state parks were full of campers. At 9:45 A.M. all mushroom hunters mustered in the Boyne City High School parking lot, from which they were to proceed, in automobile convoy, through the town and on to secret, undivulged hunting grounds. There were about a hundred cars, most of them with several mushroomers. I parked my car in one of a number of parallel rows and noticed Dana Shaler off to one side chatting confidently with a group of well-wishers. Within a few minutes the row next to mine began to fill up. I watched in my rearview mirror as a huge, ugly, rusted brown Chrysler Newport nosed its way into the space next to mine. There was a loud derisive laugh. I looked up, startled. "Don't get in my way," said Stan Boris. "I'd hate to have to make tracks up your back."

Moments later the Boyne City chief of police leaned on his car at the front of the assemblage, pulled his mike off the dashboard, and informed us of our route. "Do not stop at stop signs or stoplights. You have this right," he squawked. Sirens wailed, and whistles blew. The convoy got under way

gradually, formed into a line that must have been a mile long, and proceeded slowly through town. Store windows were painted with giant morels. Grandmoms in rockers waved from porches. Octogenarians with dripping ice cream cones stared in amazement. Kids on Schwinn bikes with baseball bats on their shoulders counted out-of-state license plates.

Ten miles later, the convoy came to a halt in a large field surrounded by wooded hills deep in the Jordan Valley State Forest. The chairman of the mushroom festival announced the rules of the contest. There were ninety minutes in which to pick mushrooms. Anyone returning after the end of the contest would be docked mushrooms. Any contestants who returned to their cars before turning in their mushrooms would be disqualified. Everyone was then issued a numbered shopping bag from which the totals would later be counted.

There was a palpable nervousness in the air. Stan Boris and Dana Shaler were on one side of the crowd, shaking and stretching their limbs like sprinters before a track meet and eyeing each other as if each were afraid the other would get out of his sight and reap some windfall harvest. A shotgun was raised and fired, signaling the start of the contest. For a brief second the action seemed frozen. Stan Boris was suspended in mid-leap, with his numbered bag at his side, like a shopper at a fire sale. Dana Shaler was pointed toward the woods and running, with his chest out, like a Keystone Kop. Then the scene dissolved and the contestants scattered, running at full speed for the hills.

The Boyne City championships are held on two consecutive days. Saturday's round was a preliminary one. On Sunday, winners of several categories were to compete against each other in the mushroom-hunting finals. The Saturday results were satisfyingly close. Dana Shaler had 426 mushrooms; Stan Boris ("It was that last one I decided to leave"), 425. Their nearest rival had 227. That night the town of Boyne City was a social whirl—a Swiss-steak-and-mushroom-gravy dinner at the Order of the Eastern Star, an all-you-can-eat ham dinner at the Veterans of Foreign Wars, and a Mushroom Hunters' Ball at the New Mogul Inn.

On Sunday the weather was cloudy and raw, and the temperature was in the mid-thirties. A somewhat reduced and subdued parade of finalists from the first round made their way to another secret location. This time it proved to be up the Thumb Lake Road behind Boyne Falls—a spot well

known, as it turned out, to camping mushroom hunters. Once again it was a hilly region of ravines and ridges covered with beech, maple, poplar, and dying elm. Again the mushroom hunters gathered in a small clearing and were issued numbered bags. Again they scattered at a shotgun blast to scour the hillsides and forests, running, bent over with their noses to the ground like bloodhounds on a scent.

But this time, although the mushroom hunters were all there, the mushrooms were not. The champions theorized later that the campers had picked them all, or that the early blacks were almost finished and the cold weather had prevented the whites from coming out in any numbers. In any case the picking was thin, and nobody got much of either kind. Stan Boris, with his flair for the dramatic gesture, came back fifteen minutes early with a disgusted look on his face and a light sack at his side. Dana Shaler came back on time with an even lighter one. An up-and-coming mushroom-hunter, Tony Williams—whom no one seemed to have noticed, and who had won the 1980 contest—weighed in with a comparatively low total of just over 200 mushrooms to take the title.

Williams explained that he had run out at full speed and at only one point had seen Boris or Shaler behind him. He had then run on even farther because, like his older rivals, he had an irrepressible instinct to stay ahead of everyone else. Williams went on to explain that he had learned mushroom hunting from his parents, who had carried him through the woods when he was a baby. He noted also that even though he had won last year's contest, Dana Shaler and Stan Boris hadn't taken him seriously. He was the new kid.

To some, who wanted a resolution to the rivalry between the two champions, the outcome of the 1981 National Mushroom Hunting Championship was unsatisfying. But to most others—especially those who had prior experience with morels—the results merely confirmed the mushroom's already formidable reputation for unpredictability. In Boyne City a bad mushroom year is almost as satisfying as a good one. The important thing, it seems, is the reminder, via the fungi, that nature is complex and that we will never fully understand it. As Gerry Boris observed of the morels, "They're never where you expect them to be, and they're always where you don't expect to find them."

POSSUM APPLES

TEXT BY JOHN MADSON · PHOTOGRAPHY BY BETH MAYNOR

My friend Jimmy Buckles had a young red-bone hound that turned out to be a persimmon dog.

He was bred for a coonhound, but what he did best was find persimmon trees. Night after night, we always ended up in some persimmon grove. Sometimes there'd be a coon in the 'simmons, but more likely there was a clutch of fat possums. Not to mention the odd skunk and occasional fox.

Now, that wasn't a stupid dog. He just believed in taking potluck—figuring that if he found some persimmons he'd likely find some action. If it was coon action, fine. But possum action or skunk action was just as good. He was finally traded for a bird dog

that sucked eggs. Not long after that, Jimmy took up golf.

You might say that hound was an all-around dog, because about every wild critter that a dog's likely to be interested in will show up in a ripening persimmon grove sooner or later. The night shift has coons, foxes, skunks, coyotes, rabbits, flying squirrels, and others. By day there may be deer, wild turkey, bobwhites, squirrels, and a host of songbirds. Squirrel hunters and coon hunters may work both shifts. Man or beast, day or night, there aren't many woods-ramblers that can pass up a treeload of ripe persimmons.

It's a southerly kind of tree, growing generally in the southeastern third of the United States and extending all through the South except the extreme tip of Florida. It doesn't look like much. A runty tree, not usually more than thirty or forty feet high, often found in thickets in old fields or in scattered clumps along weedy fencelines. There's not much about its leaves, flowers, or knobbly bark that makes it a woodlot standout. But come autumn, with leaves gone, it is laden with those little tan fruits that are irresistible to wildlife and country folk.

A ripe persimmon is about the size and shape of a slightly flattened Ping-Pong ball, with a rich, datelike flavor and aroma. The fleshy fruits ripen from late summer all

through autumn and may hang on the trees into winter. Our persimmon belongs to the genus *Diospyros,* meaning "fruit of the gods." The name fits—if the fruit is taken when it's dead ripe. Green persimmons are loaded with astringent tannins that have more pucker per pound than any other wild fruit I know of. This can change suddenly, though, and it sometimes seems that the fruit may go from sharply astringent to syrup-sweet almost overnight. Many of my country friends believe this is triggered only by a hard frost—but frost may have nothing to do with it. I've found ripe persimmons before Labor Day at least six weeks before any frosty nights in our part of southern Illinois. There are varieties and strains of wild persimmon that may ripen in early August, and some persimmon purists believe that the sweetest and most delectable fruits are those that ripen without frost.

The flavor of a ripe persimmon is tough to describe, for it's one of those wild tastes that doesn't really have any tame comparisons. "Datelike" and "figlike" probably come as close as anything. The ripe fruit isn't very appealing to look at or handle. Inside the slightly wrinkled skin is a gooey, orange-colored pulp that surrounds a number of flat, dark seeds. In color and texture the whole thing resembles a small, very rotten apple. Some ripe fruits are so soft that they are squashed by dropping from the tree. But let it be said that they taste a lot better than they look.

You'll hear that only the windfall fruit is really good eating, and that any persimmons on the tree are still too astringent to use. That's mainly so, but I regularly gather fruit that I've gently shaken from the tree and have found it to be good. It's somewhat firmer and more easily handled than the windfall fruit, and even when a hint of astringency may linger as a faint "dry" quality that shows through the sweetness, a few days will complete the ripening process at home. A working definition of "mess" is a gathering of windfall persimmons carried in the game pocket of a hunting coat. I tried that once. Never again. Our native persimmons, fully ripe, do not travel well—which is one reason they've never been big commercially. The large persimmon found in some fruit markets is an oriental variety. It isn't nearly as rich and flavorful as our smaller native species, but it can survive shipment rigors.

It's been said that the ripening process of picked persimmons can be speeded up by putting them in a sack with a ripe apple. Or, the ripening persimmons can be placed in a mesh onion or potato sack and hung near some sort of heat vent to dry. They will last almost indefinitely and make good snacks; in fact, the origin of "persimmon" is said to be the Cree *"pasiminan,"* meaning "dried fruit." A backpacker friend has spread persimmon pulp thinly and evenly on a cookie sheet and slowly oven-dried it for "fruit leather."

The orange pulp of ripe persimmon is delicious in cakes, cookies, puddings, jams, and pies. Wash the persimmons, pull off the scaly calyx at the top of each fruit, and process the whole thing through some sort of fine colander. We use a Foley Food Mill, a patent colander that can be set on the rim of a bowl and cranked. Scrape the pulp from the sides of the colander and discard the seeds each time you add the next batch of fruit. Persimmon seeds are a nuisance but have a redeeming feature. Split in half, each seed reveals a leaf embryo in the shape of a tiny "knife," "fork," or "spoon," and a southern Illinois neighbor tells us that finding one of the little spoons is a sure sign of luck.

Persimmon recipes can be found in many books on old-time country cooking, but our favorites come from the collection of our friend Ruth Ohlemeyer of Honeycut Woods, near Brighton, Illinois. It was only today that we had our first taste of Ruth's frozen persimmon roll; up until then we'd have said that lemon-glazed persimmon bars were our favorite. Except, maybe, for persimmon bread or persimmon chiffon pie. I can't decide. Years of dedicated testing are in order.

If you live in persimmon country, locate some possum apples and try these special recipes, remembering that the discovery of a new dish does more for the happiness of man than the discovery of a star.

And before the baking starts, a last word to you ladies about persimmons and us old coon hunters. Just because we may be wrinkled and homely and look like bad apples doesn't mean we aren't sweet inside, and just because we're wild doesn't mean we're useless in the kitchen. But bring us in from the woods before we're ready, and we'll be bitter about it.

PERSIMMON DELIGHTS

PERSIMMON BREAD

Sift together:

 2 cups sifted flour

 1 tsp. baking powder

 ½ tsp. salt

 1 tsp. baking soda

 1 tsp. cinnamon

 ½ tsp. nutmeg

Cream together, and gradually blend in the above ingredients:

 ½ cup shortening or oleo

 ¾ cup sugar

 2 eggs, beaten

 1 tsp. vanilla

Add last:

 1 cup persimmon pulp

 ½ cup nuts

Pour batter and persimmon/nut mixture into a well-greased 9″ x 5″ x 3″ loaf pan and let set for 20 minutes before baking. Bake 55 to 60 minutes at 375°.

LEMON-GLAZED PERSIMMON BARS

Mix and set aside:

 1 cup persimmon pulp

 1 tsp. baking soda

Combine, and mix with above:

 1 egg, beaten

 1 cup sugar

 ½ cup salad oil

 1 cup raisins

Combine, and blend with above:

 1 tsp. cinnamon

 1 tsp. nutmeg

 1½ cups flour

 ½ tsp. salt

 ¼ tsp. cloves

1 cup nuts (added last to the batter)

Spread in greased 10″ x 15″ jelly-roll pan. Bake for 20 minutes in 350° oven. Cool for five minutes and glaze.

Glaze

 1 cup confectioner's sugar

 2 tsp. lemon juice

Blend well and spread over persimmon bars.

PERSIMMON CHIFFON PIE

 1 cup persimmon pulp

 4 egg yolks

 ⅓ cup sugar

 1 envelope unflavored gelatin

 ¼ tsp. salt

Beat persimmon and egg yolks together. Mix sugar, gelatin, and salt in saucepan. Stir persimmon and egg yolks into pan. Cook and stir just until mixture comes to boil. Remove from heat. Stir occasionally until mixture mounds on a spoon.

 4 egg whites, beaten to soft peaks

 ¼ cup sugar

Add sugar to the egg whites and beat to stiff peaks. Stir in the persimmon mix, gently folding it into the beaten egg whites. Pile into a graham cracker crust. Chill.

PERSIMMON ROLL

 1 cup granulated sugar

 1 cup brown sugar

 1 lb. crushed graham crackers

 1 cup chopped pecans

 1 lb. miniature marshmallows

 2 cups persimmon pulp (added last)

Mix ingredients together in large bowl or crock. Divide into thirds, and roll each into a four-inch roll on waxed paper. Wrap roll in the waxed paper and freeze.

To serve: cut into ½-inch slices and top with whipped cream or ice cream.

IN PRAISE OF THE DANDELION

BY JONATHAN RICHARDSON

A lawn is a thing of beauty; but, if considered without prejudice, so is a dandelion.

Is it un-American to admire the archenemy? I speak of *Taraxacum officinale,* that impudent yellow face in every green carpet of grass. Surely you can't wholly hate such a spunky antagonist, especially one with the survival tricks of a Houdini. From spring to fall it performs its weekly escape act, and if a poll were taken among suburbanites to nominate the weed most impervious to lawn mowers, *Taraxacum*—the dandelion—would no doubt sweep the election.

Subversive I may be, but I can't resist applauding a species that defies man's best efforts to eradicate it. A well-manicured lawn is a thing of beauty; but, if considered without prejudice, so is a dandelion. Consequently I have never let the counterattack of *Taraxacum* ruin my weekends, though it has not always helped my mood. Who, after all, enjoys being ridiculed? And how else can one feel when, after a muscular session with the mower, one is greeted the next day by a throng of yellow faces and silver bonnets towering over the close-cropped turf?

How does this escape artist defy the guillotine? Part of its strategy is obvious at a glance. In any well-kept lawn the leaves of dandelions emerge at ground level rather than from a stalk and elude damage by lying flattened to the ground. Indeed, the more often you mow, the flatter the leaves lie. The only stalk is the naked one that hoists the flower and later the seed ball aloft.

But it is these elevated parts, reminiscent of a thumb held to an urchin's nose, that most enrage the lawn perfectionist. One Sunday, having been mocked yet again, I gave way to curiosity. How could those stalks have escaped the blade that on Friday was whirring so low? Curiosity gave rise to investigation; over the next several weeks, armed with ruler, pencil, and paper, I recorded the growth of individual stems. *Voilà!* The cleverest element in *Taraxacum's* strategy was revealed in all its simplicity.

My measurements showed that the potentially vulnerable head of a dandelion is not thrust skyward at a constant rate but in bursts. For many days after a bud appears it has no stalk at all, but nestles in its flat rosette of leaves like the centerpiece of a salad platter, well below the lowest setting of my mower. Only when the bud is ready to open does the stalk suddenly begin to grow. Then, high above its basal leaves for just a day or two, the flower advertises boldly to passing insects. When the bloom closes, the stalk cannot undo its previous growth but becomes flaccid and collapses, so that while its seeds mature, the aging flower head again lies close to the ground. A mower at this time will pass right over it again. Then the stalk stiffens and there is another spurt of growth. Within a day or two the head may be raised five or six inches, and the ripe seed ball becomes an easy target for wind (or the breath of helpful children), which disperses the seeds on their gossamer parachutes.

Thus for only two brief periods in a dandelion's growth cycle—when the flower opens and when the seeds are ready for dispersal—is it vulnerable to a marauding mower. Given a plant's need to attract pollinators and disseminate its offspring, one can scarcely imagine a more perfect strategy.

But even now a more evasive strategy is in prospect. *Taraxacum* no longer really needs insects to effect pollination; it has evolved the ability to set seed and to germinate without cross-fertilization (even, in many cases, without fertilization at all—a phenomenon known as apomixis). This being so, the first growth spurt of the stalk, the function surely making the flower conspicuous to pollinators, seems an unnecessary evolutionary anachronism. The next step in adaptation may be to delay stalk growth until after flowering when the seeds are ready for dispersal. This leaves one brief phase of vulnerability to the blade in each reproductive cycle.

Vulnerability, however, is a relative term. If a few of the many dandelions in my lawn unluckily raise their heads before I start mowing, they still have the last laugh. Decapitation is not the end, for the energy-packed root and leaves survive, and in time another bud will appear. Painstaking application of herbicides to individual plants seems the only way to produce a lawn without dandelions—and my sense of fair play

Above: Featherlike tufts that kids call parachutes help the wind disperse the seeds. Right: A dandelion sprouting. Below: A dandelion pushing through asphalt.

Next page: For only two brief periods in a dandelion's growth cycle—when the flower opens and when the seeds are ready for dispersal— is it vulnerable to a marauding mower. (Robert P. Carr photo)

134

has always deterred me from this approach. Besides, a lawn full of blackened, chemical-blasted weeds is, at least temporarily, far less attractive than a lawn full of healthy ones.

Like many other weeds, *Taraxacum* is not a native American. Its introduction may have been intentional, because dandelions were once considered useful food plants. But it is more likely that the first seeds arrived uninvited in the baggage of some unsuspecting European immigrant. Let us hope the carrier found the New World as bountiful as did the hitchhiker!

The marvelous dispersal powers of weeds couple with the travels of man to transport these plants almost everywhere one can conceive of them growing. A few years ago, while enjoying a sabbatical in Australia, I prematurely concluded that this land of isolation, famous for its distinctive flora and fauna, had managed to escape the dandelion. Of course I was mistaken. In Canberra, my sabbatical home, the climate is drier than *Taraxacum* likes, and I had arrived in the cool of midwinter. So I did not see the familiar yellow heads during my first weeks Down Under. Where did I finally find them? Where else but in the close-clipped, well-watered lawns of the American embassy!

In truth, frequent mowing is precisely the reason that dandelions are so successful in lawns. If the grass is allowed to grow tall, these ground-hugging plants will soon be shaded out, as one can appreciate by comparing their numbers in lawns and nearby unmown meadows. In a meadow one can find a few dandelions reaching for the sun as best they can—their leaves larger and no longer prostrate, their stalks longer than those in your lawn—but the competition of larger plants is not friendly to *Taraxacum*.

Doubtless the dandelion's lawn-mower strategy appeared long before the first lawn, for such a strategy also is ideal in pastures and heavily grazed natural grasslands. In an earlier, more rural America dandelions flourished primarily in barnyards and pastures. Here, as in a lawn, competing plant species are cropped short while the low-lying dandelion is spared. Indeed, certain features of *Taraxacum*—for example its toothed, thistle-mimicking leaves and bitter white sap—make sense as adaptations to grazing animals, not to mechanical grazers.

The spread of urbanization at the expense of rural America has not checked the spread of the dandelion. Indeed, its growth may be nearly as rampant as ours. For each year we create for our pretty adversary countless additional acres of the finest *Taraxacum* habitat of all—suburban lawns!

ELEGANT BUILDER OF SOUTHERN DUNES

TEXT BY EDWARD R. RICCIUTI · PHOTOGRAPHY BY LES LINE

Tall as a basketball star, tough as nails, lovely as an egret's plumes, the wild grass we call sea oats anchors the sands against wind and surf. Photos in this story were taken at the National Audubon Society's Pine Island Sanctuary, found in North Carolina.

Early September, its sun-washed days and nights that carry a hint of autumn crispness, brings squadrons of migrating red-winged blackbirds and song sparrows to the dunes that rise behind the broad, sandy beaches of North Carolina's Outer Banks. Many of the migrators alight on the fluffy, straw-colored inflorescences that top tall grasses growing in the sand of the seaward dunes. While foraging for the seeds hidden in the tufts, the birds often bow the stalks under their weight in a graceful arch toward the sand.

The grass on which the migrating blackbirds and sparrows feed is a species known as sea oats, *Uniola paniculata,* a name derived

from the oatlike appearance of its seeds. Sometimes standing as high as a professional basketball player, sea oats are also sought after by people because the drooping flower clusters, as elegant as egret plumes, can last for years in dried floral arrangements.

Rustling and swaying in the omnipresent breeze, sea oats lend a touch of life to the barren flank of dunes that face the full brunt of wave and wind. This gracile grass, however, contributes much more than its beauty. Without sea oats, the dunes would probably not exist.

The sea oats' expansive root system spreads under the surface of the beach and anchors sands that otherwise would shift ceaselessly, and so lays the foundation of the dune. The tufts, stems, and leaves intercept windblown sand, which piles up and builds the dune above the level of the beach. Sea oats stabilize the dunes, holding them together until they mature to the point at which other vegetation can achieve a foothold, further bulwarking them against the assaults of storm and sea.

Along the sandy coasts of the southeastern United States and the Gulf of Mexico, from North Carolina to Texas, sea oats, more than any other force, bind the sand of the foredunes, those that stand on the upper beach a stone's throw above the strand line. In terms of dune-building, they are the dominant plant on the shores where they grow.

Sea oats range from Cape Henry, Virginia, at the mouth of Chesapeake Bay, south to the fringes of Mexico's Yucatán Peninsula. Old records indicate that this grass once may have been spottily distributed even farther south, to Ecuador and Colombia. But modern botanists are unsure whether scientists who reported the existence of sea oats in South America during the nineteenth century confused them with one of the several other dune grasses that are their close relatives. Stands of sea oats also grace dunes throughout the Bahamas and on the northwestern coast of Cuba, but are absent from all the other islands of the West Indies.

At the northern and southern extremities of their range sea oats are sparse, and eventually they disappear among other dune grasses that take over their role as stabilizers of the sand. The geography over which sea oats grow is precisely bounded by climate; they are strictly a subtropical plant, unable to flourish where winters are severe or temperatures too warm.

The role temperature plays in determining the range of sea oats is dramatically evident along the coast of North Carolina, where scientists from North Carolina State University at Raleigh have intensively studied the plant's effectiveness as a dune-builder. The dunes of extreme southeastern Virginia and northeastern North Carolina are the only places where stands of sea oats grow alongside those of American beach grass, *Ammophila breviligulata,* which takes over as the dominant builder of dunes to the north. The normal maximum daily temperature in this area during the June-to-September growing season is about 82 degrees Fahrenheit. This region is the "natural breaking point in the southward distribution of American beach grass and northern distribution of sea oats," says North Carolina State's Ernest D. Seneca, a coastal plant ecologist.

Beach grass grows more profusely at daytime temperatures between 70 degrees F and 80 degrees F, explains Seneca; but once the mercury rises into the eighties, "its photosynthetic machinery doesn't crank up." On the other hand, says Seneca, "sea oats just begin to break even between eighty and eighty-five degrees."

In the latitude of North Carolina, sea oats flourish in midsummer but die back during the winter. Beach grass withers during the peak of summer but benefits from a longer season than sea oats because of moderating temperatures spring and fall. Newly established beach grass covers ground more quickly than sea oats, but its advantage is often short-lived. Beach grass is vulnerable to a scale insect and a fungus that sea oats resist. Once sea oats gain a foothold, moreover, they thrive sufficiently during the heat of summer to proliferate, and at the same time withstand drought better than beach grass.

Conservation agencies working to restore and preserve the sea-beaten dunes of the North Carolina coast use the two plants in tandem. They plant beach grass abundantly, scattering smaller amounts of sea oats through it. The beach grass fights a holding action against the erosion of sand by waves and wind until the sea oats proliferate and take over the defense of the dunes.

Sea oats and beach grass are invaluable to beach conservation strategies that are based on dune stabilization because few other plants can grow in the harsh oceanfront environment of the upper beach.

The smooth stem of sea oats is light but stiff enough to face the wind without snapping, while sufficiently flexible to bend before a tempest or under a bird's weight. At the same time, sea oats are not only resistant to salt but even seem to benefit from it. Laboratory experiments on seedling sea oats showed that those treated with salt spray received some sort of nutrition from it.

Once a sea oats seedling gets a foothold in the sand it quickly sinks a taproot that may reach more than six feet—some scientists say up to twelve feet—into the earth. Meanwhile it sends out a loosely knit maze of underground stems, called rhizomes, which anchor it firmly in the sand. The rhizomes extend from buds that sprout at varying angles from the base of the sea oats' stem. Those that grow from buds that are angled sharply upward break the surface and become leafy shoots, while the others form the underground network that holds the plant in place and absorbs moisture and nutrients from the sand. Water and nourishment are scarce on the beach, but the rhizome network makes up for the lack by covering a relatively large amount of ground quickly. Within a year the underground stems can extend almost six feet outward from the plant in all directions, knitting the sand of the dune together.

Critical to the formation of a dune by sea oats is a little-known, curious interplay between the seedling plant and the sand. Researchers have found that seedlings covered by a moderate amount of sand—too much has a smothering effect—prosper more than those that are exposed. The exact reasons are uncertain, although it may be that the sand insulates the tender young plant against excessive heat and dessication. At any rate, the growth stimulated by the accumulation of sand enables the plant to trap still more sand, which in turn promotes growth.

The seeds of sea oats are spread by the wind, by birds and rodents which feed on them, and probably even by the small ghost crabs that skitter along the sands of southeastern beaches. The attractive tufts that bear the flowers and ultimately the seeds are often pilfered by people who want them as decorations. Sometimes sea oats are even harvested commercially. Rangers at some national seashores must keep an eye on sea oats stands or else whole pickup truckloads may be pirated overnight. If sea oats and the other plants of that community perish, then the dunes themselves are doomed.

VI
SPECIAL PLACES

LIFE ON THE BACKSIDE OF THE MOON

BY JOHN MADSON

The day was running out, with shadows deepening in the arroyos and the late sunlight flat and orange against the pinnacles at the head of Sage Creek Basin.

For over an hour I had been trying to find a way up to the rim and out of there, and now I was scrambling down again, knowing I'd have to return by the way I'd come in, which was a very bad way. I stopped on a crumbling ledge to rest and cuss, looking out over the tortured floor of the basin toward the heights a mile to the southeast. A faint movement up there. High up, coming into the late October sunlight across a narrow, grassy table just below the crenulated skyline.

All day I had packed the 32× spotting 'scope without using it, and since early afternoon I had been wishing it was an extra canteen. Now, feeling wiser than a treeful of owls, I set up the telescope and focused on the distant ridge. The moving speck resolved into a young bighorn ram whose attention was fixed on something that moved at the edge of the 'scope's field. A ewe, grazing along the tableland fifty yards from the ram. He walked a few paces, watching her intently, then paused and looked back. A second ram appeared from somewhere below the far edge and came over to join the first. Each carried half-curve horns and still had some of the slimness of adolescence. I reckoned them to be in their fourth autumn— old enough to be interested in comely ewes but young enough to be discreet in the presence of any senior rams. They stood together, longingly watching the ewe, and then—as if on signal—both looked back down the trail.

He materialized instantly; one moment there was nothing behind the two young rams, and then the shadow behind a low spire seemed to intensify and coalesce, and a great dark ram walked slowly onto the stage. The ewe was almost fawn-colored in that light; the two young rams were darker, with

Bachelor bighorn rams in February here; old bison bull in Sage Creek Basin on previous two pages; at sunset, passing storm at Pinnacles, overleaf (photos by Ron Spomer).

145

cream-colored rump patches. The newcomer was darkest of all, almost chocolate, appearing to be twice as heavy as either of the youngsters—a barrel-bodied old herd-sire whose massive horns swept back and out, curving in a full curl with broomed tips ending on the level of his amber eyes. I had been looking for him most of the week, the principal actor in this theater of the high Badlands, and now the old ham had finally appeared with his supporting juveniles and ingenue waiting onstage, and his entrance couldn't have been more spectacular.

He stalked past the two young rams, which fell into single file behind him. The ewe gave no sign of having seen them and grazed on peacefully as the old herd-master slowly approached, stealing toward the ewe like a bird dog closing on a covey of quail that has started to move, head lowered and neck stretched to catch her scent. The two strip-

lings were close behind, taking care not to come between their chief and his lady.

The old ram made no attempt to mount the ewe; he simply bird-dogged her across the grassy tableland, keenly interested but also showing that neither he nor the ewe was quite ready for the autumn mating games and jousts of bighorn sheep. He never lost that taut alertness, and she never displayed the slightest interest. This prenuptial parade made a full circuit of the ridge before the ewe finally kicked up her heels and vanished into a ravine. The three rams walked over to a point and stood there in the waning light, the two younger animals facing the old one almost nose to nose. I've never been one to anthropomorphize, but I could almost hear the dialogue:

"Well, it's Saturday night. What's up?"

"Oh, I don't know. Would you kids like to do something?"

"Sure. What do you want to do?"

"Beats me. Anything you'd like to do?"

And so on.

The tableau lasted for twenty minutes in the lowering light. Some high cloud cover was moving in from the northwest, promising snow, and the last of the sun burnished the rich sable of the big ram as he stood with head raised while the young rams attended him, facing him as if awaiting the word. Then one of them broke away and disappeared over the far edge, followed by the other. The old herd-master walked slowly after them and went out of sight, and I figured that was the last of it. But a minute later he reappeared on a grassy table far below, splendid head held high, in an airy, weightless trot that took him into the gathering darkness.

I did the same, but less gracefully and at considerable cost to my outfit, scrambling, sliding, and tearing out the seat of my patched Levis. When I finally got to the road it was full dark, which was okay, considering the state of my pants. Dust-dry, scuffed and spavined, but still exulting in the sight of those splendid animals and secure in the hope that there'd be lambs next spring in hidden nurseries high in the pinnacles.

The little herd of bighorns in South Dakota's Badlands National Park needs all the lambs it can get. The herd hasn't done all that well since wild sheep were stocked there twenty years ago.

Twenty-two bighorns were brought into the old Badlands National Monument and held in an enclosed pasture for several years, and after half the sheep died of disease in 1967 the survivors were set free. Today, the National Park Service puts the herd at about forty animals, although there are probably more than that; about a year ago wildlife photographer Ron Spomer was in the highest, most rugged part of the park's north unit and counted forty-five bighorns in one band. No one can be sure of the real total. Small groups of the sheep travel widely. Some have been reported as far south as Stronghold Table in the southern unit of the park and as far east as the rough breaks near the town of Kadoka—an extreme spread of at least sixty miles. Most of these far-ranging sheep appear to be young rams, the "social castrates" of the main population, but one bighorn seen near Kadoka was an older animal. As far as anyone knows there are three dominant rams in the herd—two with at least a three-quarter curl of horn, and the big full-curl ram.

The Badlands' bighorn population appears stable. Too stable. National Park Service biologist Hank McCutchen feels the sheep aren't expanding as they should, and

the cause is hard to nail down. Food is in good supply. Hank has found plenty of "ice cream" forage species that the sheep have hardly used. Is there any evidence of climbing injuries on the treacherous Badlands formations? No. He's found nothing to indicate that. Something, though, is wrong with lamb survival. Hank has seen flocks that might include eight or ten lambs but only a few yearlings. It appears that many lambs aren't getting past their first winter. Disease, possibly. He has found a low incidence of lungworm in the droppings of both adults and lambs, and suspects that lungworm larvae are being transmitted through the placentas and infecting lambs before birth.

Another problem is suitable water supply. There is less water in the Badlands than there once was; overgrazing and farming have sapped the old aquifers, and many of the original springs have dried up or been silted in. If existing waterholes are very far from escape terrain (and a couple of hundred yards can be too far) and there's cover capable of concealing coyotes, predation on young sheep can be serious. There is no firm evidence of eagle predation. There is a recent case of a mature ram being shot by a poacher, but the general behavior of the sheep doesn't show the spookiness usually reflected in a hunted population. Adding it all up, McCutchen feels that the major limiting factor of bighorns in Badlands National Park is probably one of the distribution and condition of watering places.

These sheep are of Rocky Mountain stock, replacing the extinct Audubon bighorn—the subspecies that may have been the largest of all our North American wild sheep. Audubon reported a ram that weighed 344 pounds, of which horns and skull alone weighed 44.5 pounds. Variously called "Audubon bighorn," "Badlands bighorn," and "Black Hills bighorn," the type locality for this sheep was generally in the Badlands between the Cheyenne and White rivers.

It's been said that the Audubon bighorn's last stand was in the Black Hills, where it was wiped out around 1895. However, some records go well beyond that. A Badlands hunter named Charley Jones shot a ram on Sheep Mountain Table just south of the little town of Scenic in 1903. Some bighorns still ranged on and around Sheep Mountain Table in 1908 and 1909 but were last recorded there in 1910. However, there's an old photo of a professional wolf hunter standing before his tent with a typical Badlands "wall" in the background. Captioned "fresh meat in camp," it shows the head, foreparts, and dressed hindquarters of a bighorn sheep

Mule deer bucks in Sage Creek Basin, early October, with Hay Table rising in the distance (Ron Spomer).

149

hanging from the meat pole. This may have been the animal killed about 1918 between Big and Little Corral draws, just west of Sheep Mountain Table.

That was about it. But in 1926, several miles southwest of Camp Crook, South Dakota, near the breaks of the Little Missouri, a lone bighorn ram was shot. And while it's possible that ram may have wandered up the Little Missouri from the North Dakota Badlands, the chances of its having come from bighorn country farther west are considered remote. Veteran South Dakota game biologists strongly suspect that this ram—which was known locally and diligently hunted by ranchers for several years—was the last of its race. *Sic transit auduboni.*

The big stuff went early. Bison once used the Badlands for summer range, but a severe three-year drought that began in 1861 put a temporary end to that. By the time the drought finally broke, the bison had been pushed farther west by hunting pressure, and they never did return in any real numbers.

For a skilled professional of the 1870s, market hunting for the Black Hills gold camps could be more profitable than mining. And compared with other early western mining regions, the Black Hills and adjacent Badlands must have provided relatively easy picking. The valleys of the White and Cheyenne rivers were among the best hunting grounds, and the deer, elk, bighorns, and antelope of the Badlands were hard hit, early on.

Elk were abundant in the Badlands until about 1877, but during that summer hunters for the mining camps killed large numbers. When the surviving elk migrated just east of Rapid City that fall, miners and townspeople "turned out en masse and slaughtered hundreds." Their herds depleted and their old migration pattern shattered, the Badlands elk never really returned.

Black bears and grizzlies were mostly gone by the turn of the century, and wolves weren't far behind. The big plains "loafers" were anathema to stockmen, who paid bounties of $5 to $20 for each old wolf and $3 for pups, and sometimes gave free room and board to the wolf hunter. A big spread with a predation problem might even hire a wolfer by the month, paying $50 per month and board. On top of that, the State of South Dakota paid a bounty of $5 for each adult wolf and $2 for a pup. What with one thing and another, a good wolfer might make better wages than a top cowhand.

The grizzly bear and gray wolf never really returned to the Badlands—and for a long time not much of anything else was there either. A 1919 survey revealed little wildlife in the Badlands and concluded, "The entire region seems void of all wild animal life."

When I first saw the South Dakota Badlands in 1929, the year they were named a national monument, wildlife was still at a low ebb. There were a few deer in the wilder corners but no bighorns or bison and not many pronghorn antelope. With national monument status and the emergence of modern wildlife conservation, though, things began to pick up. Antelope were trickling back into the Badlands during the early 1940s but were still rare. Into the 1950s and 1960s pronghorns continued to build, drifting freely in and out of the Badlands and steadily increasing. In 1963 they were joined by their old plains partners when a herd of fifty-three bison was stocked in the western part of the monument. The buffs settled in, found it to their liking, and prospered. Within five years the original herd had increased threefold, putting new life into the Tyree and Sage Creek basins. Every now and then they put some spice into my life, too.

A "table" in Badlands parlance is simply a flat-topped mesa with vertical sides. Some are hundreds of acres; others are only a few feet across. Most are perfectly flat and covered with grass. On overnight trips into the western basins of the Badlands I coveted certain little tables that were maybe thirty feet in diameter with sheer sides. In buffalo country this makes for a feeling of security and a sound night's sleep. At least, it used to. Several winters ago I backpacked alone into the Tyree Basin during a period of relatively deep snow. I set up camp on a Badlands table no larger than my living room at home. It was five feet high with no breaks in its sheer sides—an unassailable bastion. I'd seen fresh buffalo trails on the way in, but they'd never follow me up on that table, right? Wrong.

Deep-winter camping alone is a great way to catch up on sleep. There's no one to talk to, and I can't say I enjoy reading in a sub-zero tent. So that evening I dined early, was in my sleeping bag by 6:00 P.M., and slept the clock around. Stepping out into a dazzling sunrise I found a neat line of buffalo tracks around my tent. Sometime during the night a curious buff had found me there, scaled the vertical bank, looked things over, and politely exited over the far side without waking me. I still camp on those little tables because they're floor-flat and comfortable, but I do so with no illusions.

When I travel up the south side of the Sage Creek Basin at the edge of the main buffalo range I always have binoculars, for I like to stop frequently and check the landscape for signs of company. This south ridge is a favorite hangout for solitary buffalo bulls that may be half-hidden by a fold of land or a clump of trees. I like to know when they're on my line of march. It's rude to startle them, and I'm the soul of courtesy to a cranky old buffalo bull.

I was returning to camp along that upland one fine afternoon, checking the route ahead as I usually do, and saw a lone buffalo skylined about a mile ahead. I noted the location and altered course to give him a wide berth. But there were two deep drainages to cross, and the second one forced me off my course. As I topped out I was distracted by a gleaming slope of polished chalcedony pebbles and didn't have buffalo in mind.

Passing within fifty feet of some junipers, I heard a deep groan. In the shadow between two of the trees stood a huge, black, frowning stormcloud of a bull buffalo. Again, that deep groan. His head was slowly going down and his tail was slowly coming up, and he was beginning to look downright uncharitable. He was 2,000 pounds of growing unhappiness, but he wasn't any unhappier than I was. The nearest cover was another clump of junipers about 400 yards down the open ridge. It was one of my longer walks. There was no point in running; that might have triggered him, and there's no outrunning a buffalo. When last seen he was still frowning down the hillside at me and rumbling curses. A bland little adventure, looking back at it. I guess you had to be there.

There are several hundred buffalo in the Badlands. The number varies. A few years back, when there were about 450, they began breaking out of the park boundaries into pastures and wheatlands north and west of the park. This incursion was frowned upon by ranchers. The herd was summarily reduced; the surplus was shipped down to the Pine Ridge Indian Reservation for the Oglala Sioux herd. And twenty-two miles of high, strong, reasonably buffalo-tight fence was put up along the north and west sides of the Sage Creek Basin. In the fall of 1983 park officials estimated the bison count to be 370, mostly cows with about fifty calves and fifty mature bulls. Their general health is very good, and the herd went into the winter of 1983 with modest numbers and an immoderate amount of good forage. But water is always something of a range problem in the Badlands, and some of the old catch basins at the head of Sage Creek are being blasted out, deepened, and their capacity doubled.

Mixed in with the bison is an ephemeral

population of pronghorn antelope that range through much of the Badlands as single animals, small bunches, or herds of a hundred or more. Highly mobile, they come and go. Mule deer are much the same, although they tend to be more sedentary than pronghorns. Last fall, as I skirted the north side of the Conata Basin, I happened to notice some clumps of sumac several hundred yards away in a field of deep grass—a singular thing, seeing as how sumac didn't belong there. I climbed a little formation and glassed the situation, and deer began to sprout out of the grass. Four were very large bucks whose antlers accounted for the "sumac." There were eight others, too—an even dozen mule deer bucks having a bachelor party before the rise of the rutting moon.

Antelope and bison are two sides of the same coin. They are grasslanders that flourish together. Mule deer are another matter. They may not do well in plains country with high bison populations that often forage and bed down in the brushy draws on which muleys

Winter afterglow in Pinnacles, with bison in foreground (Jim Brandenburg).

depend for browse and cover. This probably had a lot to do with the early distribution of deer on the Great Plains. But in the big basins on the west side of Badlands National Park the two species have struck an ecological bargain—and on a day when I've counted two hundred bison I have also seen as many as twenty mule deer.

Badlands deer and antelope appear to be in excellent physical shape—thanks in no small part to steady pressure by predators. With wolves gone there's not much that can work on the buffalo, but the Badlands have coyotes aplenty, and the little songdogs prey on young antelope and deer when they can. The Badlands are one of the few places I've heard coyotes singing in the middle of the day, and their sign can be found almost anywhere up in the big formations that a person can climb. I've yet to see bobcats in the Badlands, although I've seen their tracks. But in recent years there have been several reports of Little Bob's big cousin. Three mountain lion cubs were seen playing on one of the main roads in 1963, and the U.S. Fish and Wildlife Service has reported an adult cougar east of the park in the Kadoka area.

There's no one I'd rather be with in the deep Badlands than Bill Lone Hill. A former tribal policeman on the huge Pine Ridge Indian Reservation, and a park ranger for fifteen years, Bill knows the Badlands National Park like his own backyard—which it is, come to think of it.

One evening when he and his family lived near the White River Visitor Center in the south unit, Bill heard a woman crying for help from beside the road. He looked around, calling out but getting no reply. He searched again next day, helped by a nearby road crew, but they found nothing. He had nearly forgotten the incident several days

Prairie rattlesnake found on Badlands rim (Gary Withey).

later when he was hiking along the White River north of his house. Coming back by a different route he paused on some high ground above the river. Down below, walking along the bank and unaware of Bill's presence, was a full-grown mountain lion. Later that day some boys came tearing up to Bill's headquarters saying they had seen a "huge cat" while swimming in the river. They had dressed en route, which isn't easy on motor bikes.

If there's a winged counterpart of the mountain lion, it's the golden eagle. This magnificent raptor frequents the Badlands, nesting and hunting there, and investing the stark landscapes with a mysticism that isn't lost on the Sioux.

One day Bill Lone Hill and I were deep in the "baddest of the Badlands" between the village of Red Shirt and Stronghold Table when a golden eagle soared over us, the white rondels of its underwings marking it as a youngster. While we watched it off into the north, Bill told of a funeral he'd attended not long before. A middle-aged man, a devotee of the Old Ways, had insisted on dancing in an annual pow-wow in spite of a heart condition and his doctor's warnings. But the ceremony meant too much to him to give up—and in his final dance he had made but one circle when he fell dead.

Dying as he did during the ceremonial, he was given a traditional Sioux funeral that embodied many of the old customs. There was a four-day waiting period between the time of death and the funeral, with burial at the dancing grounds, and there was a basket of gift turquoise and silver to which the people helped themselves. It was spring, and during the funeral a pair of golden eagles swung high overhead. That was impressive enough, but even more stirring was the sound of the eagles screaming—something few of the people had ever heard, and which was regarded as highly significant. A person may live for years in golden eagle country and never hear one scream—but then, it isn't every day that such a dancer passes on.

Golden eagle predation on young bighorns, antelope, and deer fawns is probably nominal at most, although you'll hear heated claims to the contrary through much of the West. Little is known of eagle predation on big game in the Badlands, although the huge birds are capable of preying successfully on fawns and antelope kids. Author Joy Hauk tells of a Badlands eagle that took on a grown coyote and actually lifted the songdog off the ground. Both fell to earth and faced each other in a standoff until the coyote's nerve failed and he lit out for a nearby fence

where he cowered behind a post until the eagle had gone. You can't really blame that coyote; a free golden eagle is an awesome thing. I was walking along the north rim of Sage Creek Basin one wild spring day, a few hundred yards from a large prairie dog town, when I flushed a golden eagle that had been perched just over the edge out of the wind. The great bird turned downwind and passed close by on wings spanning almost eight feet, and if there'd been a fencepost to hide behind I'd have damn well gone for it.

Much as I admire such majesty, though, my favorite Badlands birds are far more modest. In the deepest part of winter along the windswept roads, clouds of snow buntings whirl into the air—their shadings of white and light brown a perfect match to the landscape. In high summer, long after the buntings have gone to the Arctic, the Badlands are set with sapphires. I've never been in the main campground near park headquarters during the warm months when there weren't Rocky Mountain bluebirds in attendance. A half-dozen or more may be in sight at one time, and on sunny days they are that fine shade of deep blue that you'll see in Badlands sunsets, just above the bands of salmon and gold.

The abiding horror of many Badlands visitors is the prairie rattlesnake, which probably keeps some people on the roads and off the trails. The irony of this is that the Big Badlands, by and large, are a good place to get away from rattlesnakes. I've seen fewer rattlers within the park than in South Dakota range country as a whole. Most of the Badlands is just too barren for rattlesnakes, with neither cover nor food. The few rattlers I've seen in the park were either in prairie dog towns or heavy grass, but never in the bare

formations themselves. Anyway, the threat of rattlesnakes shouldn't keep anyone out of those fine backlands. The more you're in rattler country the more you accept snakes as a fact of life—like cactus and gyp water. At the risk of being struck, stuck, or fluxed, you live with such things but don't take liberties with them.

Prairie rattlers have a reputation for being on the hot side as rattlesnakes go, and it's true that they can be touchy. But the only really het-up prairie rattler I've seen was the one that Bob "He-Dog" Henderson grabbed barehanded as it was escaping down a prairie dog hole. He-Dog hauled it out by the tail and tossed it aside. Hot? That snake was plumb incandescent.

Sometimes, however, the forbearance of a prairie rattler surpasseth all understanding. Like one that a friend of ours brought into Scenic.

The social center of that little Badlands village was the infamous Longhorn Saloon, which was owned by "Halley" Merrill, who looked like Buffalo Bill's uncle. The real tough uncle. There were bullet holes in the ceiling and sawdust on the floor—to soak up the blood, some said. Anyway, my friend Jim Brandenburg brought this big prairie rattler to town one summer afternoon and turned it loose in front of the Longhorn. The cowboys tried to stir it up, but it was a sleepy sort of day and the snake wasn't mad at anybody. In the prevailing spirit of conviviality, someone offered to buy the rattler a drink. They took the snake inside and put it on the bar and tried to interest it in some beer. The rattlesnake couldn't be corrupted. It wouldn't drink and it wouldn't fight, so it plainly didn't belong in the Longhorn. Jim turned it loose just outside of town, figuring it might

Common nighthawk photographed near Norbeck Pass (Ron Spomer).

155

Above: Black-tailed prairie dog, Sage Creek (Gary Withey). Next page: Seven bighorn rams on slopes leading to Hay Table (Ron Spomer).

start a whole line of highly moral rattle-snakes.

"And we can but hope," he told the waddies back at the saloon, "that the example shown by that noble buzztail will not be lost on certain unrefined, bowlegged, White River brush-poppers I could name."

The backlands. Those parts away from roads, out back of beyond, behind the post-card pictures in those special reaches of the Badlands that our friend Curt Twedt calls "the Goodlands."

There are many ways to go, from the short walks and well-marked longer paths (mostly in the eastern part of the park) to the trails that grow dimmer as they fade into wilderness, pointing to places where you make your own tracks and follow no one's lead. There's a way for everyone; the main thing is to get out of your car and away from the parking lot if you can. The Park Service schedules guided "nature walks" during the tourist season, and the ones I've taken have been excellent. They usually last several hours, leaving shortly after dawn to avoid midday heat and often leading in, through, and over some fine Badlands. If you are gimpy, though, ask about these hikes in advance. They have their rough spots.

For a few, the best trails of all are the skeined game trails that wander up and over the "tables" and through the passes, into lost canyons and up onto cedared shelves.

The best times for such doings are in spring and fall when temperatures are moderate, tourists are fewer, and the midday light is better for photography than in full summer. I've packed into the Badlands in all seasons and known July days of 104 degrees F and February nights of –15 degrees F and have enjoyed it all, though I'll freely admit that late October is hard to beat. High summer presents problems. Getting into some of the best backlands may require a long day—and that means at least a gallon of water. If you plan to be active in early afternoon when the sun is thrown back by those beige walls and the breathless canyons swim with heat, consider taking two gallons per person per day. There's no drinkable water back there unless you pack a purification outfit and share a waterhole with buffalo.

This matter of water is why I like to leave camp very early and come in at sundown in midsummer—spending the middle of the day shut down on some high shelf under a canopy of cedars. Might as well. Most critters are shut down, too, and the light is bad for pictures. So relax in a pool of deep shade, looking out into the white blaze of a Badlands afternoon and listening to pure silence.

Take off your boots and dry your socks. Have an apple. Sooner or later, something will develop. As it did one day when I was sharing a fine loafing-place with some pale Badlands chipmunks and happened to glance at a patch of bare ground only a few feet away. The place was an on-site museum of Oligocene fossils. Scattered over several square yards were fragments of ancient turtle shell that looked like shards of terra-cotta pottery. A closer look revealed bone fragments and teeth of an oreodont—a sheep-sized mammal that grazed here in herds thirty million years ago. Nearby was part of a lower jaw, teeth in place, tinted a shade of cinnamon and clearly defined in its matrix of light Badlands clay. A private exhibit and a transient one, for the fossils were already deteriorating with exposure.

I leave such things in place, rarely even touching them anymore. Not because I don't hanker after curios, for I do, nor just because it's unlawful to take fossils from federal lands, which it is. But an Oligocene mammal bone in place has a quality that it loses when disinterred. Out of place its aura of great antiquity begins to fade, and with it vanishes that faint perception of a remote and unpeopled world. Any mystery or message is lost. The fossil becomes just a lump of minerals. So I leave the turtle shells and oreodont teeth as I find them, interred in their monuments of richly tinted alluvia and volcanic ash. I can offer them nothing better.

Much as I like prowling around in these high formations—and especially along the trackless eaves that overlook the Conata and Sage Creek basins—I'm often nervous about it. Not of falling from a high wall, necessarily, but of getting stuck in a hole.

Badlands sediments erode in odd ways, with rainfall draining almost unchecked to cut tunnels and caves, deep vertical trenches, and treacherous sinkholes. One summer afternoon last year I was climbing along Deer Haven at the head of the Conata Basin. This is a "slump" where high ground has collapsed to form a rough, semicircular shelf forested with juniper, and although I'm familiar with most of it, I had never been over on a grassy eastern part. I worked over that way, farther than I'd ever gone, tramping blithely across an open plateau. Then I began noticing odd holes almost hidden in the heavy grass. Some were like animal burrows a foot or two in diameter; just beyond were pits twenty feet across, constricting funnel-like in their depths. I was at the edge of the worst before I ever saw it—a hidden sinkhole only four feet in diameter but perhaps ten times that deep. A fearsome place and a terrible thing for a lone hiker to step into. Cliffs, and the possibility of falls, I can face. But I can't handle the thought of stepping into one of those pits while alone and being wedged deep out of sight and hearing. Next time up there, I'm packing a climber's ax.

Getting back into the stark, flayed mazes of the Big Badlands is mandatory for anyone loving good boondocks, but most of the wildlife action occurs through the grasslands of the big tables and the main basins. The heart of this is an eight-by-twelve-mile designated wilderness that embraces the Sage Creek and Tyree basins and is best entered from the primitive campground at its northwest corner. If you keep to high ground south of Sage Creek Basin it's reasonably good walking without having to fight past some of those godawful Badlands arroyos. And while I don't usually keep careful head counts, in the course of one long day above Sage Creek I've seen buffalo, antelope, mule deer, sharptailed grouse, a prairie falcon, a golden eagle, a rattlesnake, bluebirds, turkey buzzards, magpies, a sprinkling of prairie dogs, a coyote, and a badger on his way home after a hard night. During that particularly fine September day there were no other hikers. At any time of year I seldom meet anyone in the remote Badlands. Not that I crave company back there, but something about this bothers me, and it's a note to close on.

The people I do meet are almost invariably on the sunny side of thirty, full of prance and the strong juices of youth. Now and then I'll meet a youngster of forty or so, but it's been years since I've seen anyone my own age in the backcountry, and I sometimes wonder about the boys and girls I used to play with. Where are they, now that our hair is white? I've only to go to the main campground to find out. They'll be there overnight on their way to Mount Rushmore, in air-conditioned mobile homes looking at pictures of grandchildren and "Love Boat" reruns. All those years while I've been out playing they have been growing up, Growing Substantial, and growing old.

Our ways must have parted forty-five years ago when I got into the Big Badlands, down under the Wall, for the first time. It was a stunning adventure that left me with a clear choice: to get on with the business of growing up and put such places behind me, or to remain fourteen years old and never really leave them at all.

So. See you in the backlands. I'll be the silver-tipped kid with ragged pants and an extra candy bar. Stop and talk. I've learned some good places.

VII

THE ARTIST AND NATURE

MR. AUDUBON'S LAST HURRAH

BY MICHAEL HARWOOD

The painting on the previous pages by Roy Grinnell shows John James Audubon between the Yellowstone and Missouri rivers, watching as his friends chased and killed buffalo bulls. He was only fifty-eight that summer of 1843, but his hair was white, his beard nearly so, and he had just lost the last of his teeth. And he felt old. He couldn't work at his drawings for as long at a stretch. He wasn't spry or alert enough any longer for such high-spirited, dangerous hunts. For the first time in his life he was literally a tenderfoot, vulnerable to blisters. Besides, this expedition up into the western fur country—his last expedition, which should have been the climax of his life—had disappointed him. He had expected to travel far beyond this spot, to go up the Yellowstone to the Rockies. Instead he and his scientific party were forced to remain near the mouth of the Yellowstone. He was conscious of his life slipping away with work unfinished, sights not seen. And the primitive America he had loved and written about was also slipping away.

March 11th, 1843. An hour before midnight, the celebrated nature artist and author John James Audubon and three assistants step off a train in Philadelphia, where they are met by Audubon's long-time friend and patron Edward Harris, up from Moorestown, New Jersey. Harris completes the party that will go to the Far West to draw and collect wildlife. This expedition has been mounted largely for the sake of the new work on quadrupeds Audubon is producing in collaboration with his friend the Reverend John Bachman. But it will also add to Audubon's latest publication about birds—what he calls "the small work," the octavo edition of *The Birds of America,* which will run to seven volumes, combining his bird essays with small lithographed reproductions of the double-elephant folio engravings. And, like any good natural history expedition, this one will also collect other curiosities, including geological specimens and observations.

Harris is a forty-four-year-old amateur naturalist and paying partner on this trip. He has been a member of Audubon's inner circle for nearly twenty years, and Audubon cherishes him like a brother. Harris is introduced to Lewis Squires, a young neighbor of the Audubons in Carmansville, north of New York City, who will serve as expedition secretary. Then he shakes hands with John Graham Bell, a well-known New York City taxidermist, not quite thirty-one years old, hired as the expedition's curator of specimens, and then with the slender, reticent Isaac Sprague, also in his early thirties. Sprague is an exceptionally talented natural history artist. He will go on to illustrate various botanical works by Asa Gray, including the famous *Manual of Botany,* and on this expedition he will be Audubon's assistant artist. A few years ago, during a selling trip, Audubon visited Sprague's home in Hingham, Massachusetts, hoping to meet him. Sprague was not there, but Audubon saw and greatly admired some of Sprague's bird drawings

and wrote notes on two of the drawings, telling Sprague so. Sprague has never before been on an extended scientific expedition or even camped out, so this is a major adventure for him—and, if the truth be known, somewhat daunting. The men are to travel over the Appalachian Mountains, down the Ohio River, up the Mississippi River to St. Louis, and then, as guests aboard a fur-traders' steamboat, up the Missouri River, deep into fur country and Indian country, all the way to the Yellowstone River, and perhaps from there as far as the Rocky Mountains.

Another young man, whom Audubon tried to convince to join the expedition, isn't able to come, apparently because his mother and his friends fear the dangers of the trip. He is young Spencer Fullerton Baird of Carlisle, Pennsylvania, future secretary of the Smithsonian Institution, a natural-science prodigy still in his teens. He has been corresponding with his hero Mr. Audubon for nearly three years and sending him specimens of birds and quadrupeds.

March 14th and 15th. In a bad snowstorm the party crosses the Alleghenies by stagecoach. The stage company has charged them thirty dollars for excess freight. Audubon complains this is a "first-rate piece of robbery," but they have brought with them more than half a ton of baggage, including nine trunks and assorted bags, gun cases, guns, and Harris' pointer, Brag. The snow collects to the depth of two feet in the mountains, and they are nine hours late reaching Wheeling, Virginia, on the Ohio. "This is the hardest ride I ever have had," writes Isaac Sprague, "having been now two nights with scarce any sleep."

March 28th. The steamer *Gallant*—the "filthiest of all filthy rat-traps I ever travelled in," says Audubon—arrives in St. Louis. It is carrying not only the party of naturalists but about one hundred fifty "Buckeyes, Wolverines, Suckers, Hoosiers, and gamblers, with drunkards of each and every denomination, their ladies and babies of the same nature, and specifically the dirtiest of the dirty"—so Audubon writes in what he describes as "a long and comical" letter to a friend in New York. He expects the friend to send it to the newspapers; there's no harm in keeping the name Audubon before the public. Most of these passengers apparently are settlers headed for the Missouri frontier or farther west, with their horses and wagons "and furniture of all description." Their five-day passage from Louisville has been enlivened by two brushes with disaster, one when the *Gallant* hit a submerged tree and the second when it engaged in a race with another steamer and the two boats hooked bows by mistake.

St. Louis, Audubon writes his family, "is a large town with about 20,000 inhabitants and looks well from the River, but the streets are somewhat narrow and houses rather low ... There are great numbers of steamers at the *Levee* ... They are bound for all portions of the Western World but the River is too low at present for most of them." Too low and too full of ice. They will have to wait for the spring rains, and travelers bound up the Mississippi and the Missouri will also have to wait for the breakup of the ice north of St. Louis.

April. While his companions are off on the other side of the river on an extended collecting excursion, Audubon remains in St. Louis, preparing for the trip to the Yellowstone. He accepts many invitations to dinner and is treated like a proper celebrity. (The superintendent of Indian affairs makes him an astonishing gift, one of the manuscript volumes of Lewis and Clark's expedition journal.) He receives guests and talks to dozens of men familiar with the country he is about to visit. He also shows his samples of the first illustrations for *The Viviparous Quadrupeds of North America* in hopes that someone will subscribe (no one does), and buys supplies for the expedition. He collects several specimens, dead and alive, of a common pouched rat that infests all the gardens in the area, makes his drawing of the species from these models, and observes the living rats long

A busy morning along Front Street and the levee in St. Louis, Missouri, as depicted by artist J. C. Wild in 1840 (Missouri Historical Society).

Original watercolor drawings by John James Audubon of the wolverine. Audubon apparently never saw a wolverine in the wild—even then they were mostly an Arctic and montane species. (American Museum of Natural History)

enough to write in triumph, "I now know more about the Habits of Pouched Rats than any man that has ever lived!"

He is interviewed and assayed by journalists. His "step is elastic, and he seems to have all the ardor and vigor of youth," reports one of them. Says another, "He is a man of robust constitution though not of stout frame. He told me he had not taken a particle of medicine for twenty years. He is capable of any fatigue; can walk thirty-five miles a day with ease, for months; can sleep anywhere in the open air; endure all climates... He says he can live a hundred years with temperate habits, regularity, and attention to diet."

This is vintage Audubon, buoyant and stretching the truth about himself. Actually, the nineteen years he spent working full throttle on the *The Birds of America* and the accompanying five volumes of text took a lot out of him. "I conceive myself growing old very fast," he had said ten years earlier. "So much travelling exposure and fatigue do I undergo, that the Machine me thinks is wearing out." For the last few years he has been getting his exercise mostly by "battering the pavements," as he says, personally hawking his books and his engravings to potential customers in cities from Canada to the Carolinas. He hasn't done any concentrated fieldwork since the summer of 1837, when he

went to Texas. So he's out of condition. He's also had his spells of sickness, and John Bell is carrying a scribbled prescription dictated to him by a physician friend of Audubon's in Baltimore: what to give Mr. Audubon when he has diarrhea—a pea-sized piece of camphor in a wine-glass of brandy; repeat until it takes effect.

The trouble is, from the beginning Audubon has treated the whole quadrupeds project with the same kind of unrealistic optimism he shows in that St. Louis newspaper interview. After having struggled for so many years with the birds of North America—several hundred different species—he has had the idea that the less numerous quadrupeds will present a much easier task, particularly since he is sharing the job with his two sons, Victor and John, and with John Bachman. He and the boys are doing the drawings and paintings, then publishing the engravings in groups of five plates and selling them by subscription, just as they did with the birds. Bachman is a Lutheran minister in Charleston, South Carolina, who is also an accomplished amateur mammalogist and knows the published literature well. He will produce the text, using their combined notes, and that will be published separately.

"My Hair [is] grey, and I am growing old, but what of this?" Audubon wrote to "friend Bachman" as they made their plans in 1840. "My spirits are as enthusiastical as ever, my legs fully able to carry my body for some Ten Years to come, and in about Two of these I expect to see the Illustrations out, and ere the following Twelve Months have elapsed, their Histories studied, their descriptions carefully prepared, and the Book printed!" This year of 1843 would have been the year of fulfillment if he had been a good prophet, but the project is only started.

Bachman has tried to rein Audubon in: "Don't flatter yourself that this Book is child's play—the birds are a mere trifle compared to this." Most birds move around a good deal and do so in daylight and above ground, but most mammals spend large parts of their lives either hiding in holes or prowling at night. So Audubon and Bachman, even with a large network of friends helping collect mammals for them, may miss some species altogether and will often be unable to study and describe behavior well.

They also have difficult decisions to make about which animal forms are true species and which are only local varieties or races. The scientific study of North American quadrupeds is not even as far advanced as American ornithology was when Audubon began observing and drawing birds—and that was pretty rudimentary. Having plowed through the available literature on North American animals, Bachman has spoken grimly of "the confused mass into which our quadrupeds have been thrown." He has summed up the problem for Audubon: "The skulls & teeth must be studied—& colour is as variable as the wind—down, down in the earth they grovel & in digging & studying we grow giddy & cross."

Of the two of them Bachman is the better educated in science and is the more careful and deliberate in his intellectual habits, and their friendship is a sort of forge in which Audubon's scientific ideas have been refined and shaped. But Bachman himself can be

The swift fox also painted by Audubon, who found this western species on the Missouri River expedition and brought a live specimen home with him. The swift fox has a reputation for amazing fleetness of foot, but during a buffalo hunt in 1843, Edward Harris, mounted on an Indian pony, accidentally startled one from its burrow, chased it, and easily overtook it. "Now who will tell me that no animal can compete with this Fox in speed...?" exulted Audubon. (American Museum of Natural History)

The shy Isaac Sprague drew various landscapes and natural history subjects for Audubon on the 1843 expedition, but his reputation stems largely from his later botanical work for Asa Gray. (Courtesy of Hunt Institute, Carnegie-Mellon University, Pittsburgh)

overly optimistic. Like Audubon, he has extremely high hopes for this one western expedition.

Audubon has received a letter from him in which Bachman has rattled off a string of instructions—the stay-at-home naturalist pinned to his parish and worrying that his experienced colleague will forget how to work in the field. Collect and skin birds, said Bachman. Collect reptiles and seeds and plants. But above all, "attend to your business which is looking after quadrupeds and knowing all about them, about their history. I need not say I know nothing of western animals but what the books tell me and the few I saw in confinement. Everything, therefore, you write about them will be new."

That's pretty nearly right. Very few naturalists have traveled in fur country yet, and what has been written about the mammals barely scratches the surface of the subject. Even men who have spent most of their lifetimes on the northern prairies and in the mountains know relatively little. There are a great many fur-country veterans in St. Louis, and Audubon finds them "all shockingly ignorant out of their course of Business. No one knows one animal from another beyond a Beaver, a Bear, a Raccoon, or an Otter."

Make good notes, Bachman urged in his letter, and make them daily. Measure and weigh everything before skinning, tag the specimens with information as to sex and locale, and save all the skulls. Use plenty of arsenic on the skins, to keep them free of insects. Draw animals alive whenever possible. Keep specimens of every form of animal, even those supposedly common in the East. "You know my theory—that every species except a few bats and a single species each of bear and deer is new in the Far West." Then he devoted a long paragraph to various genera and species that needed particular attention: bats, shrews, bears, badgers, weasels, martens, mink, otters, beavers, coyotes, Indian dogs, wolves, hares, meadow mice, lemmings, squirrels, elk, buffalo, mountain goats, mountain sheep, antelope.

April 17th. Audubon has been daydreaming and worrying about his wife and his sons and their families, who are all at the small family estate, Minnie's Land, on the east bank of the Hudson. Victor and John named the place after their mother, Lucy, Minnie being the Scottish diminutive for Mother. "Your last letter is dated April the 3rd (Sunday) Thermometer at 34 but clear," Audubon writes; "and I was rendered Happy by reading nearly one half in the hand writing of my own sweet and beloved sweetheart...I do sincerely hope that Victor will be able to meet all his money calls, without *ever* pledging Minnie's Land. To this latter case I never would give my consent under any circumstances *Whatever*." The Audubons are frequently in financial difficulty. Papa is famous, all right, but that hasn't made him rich. And the only way he knows to try to keep the family afloat is to publish more engravings and more books, and then go off selling them. That's one reason he has undertaken the quadrupeds project.

"I think you have had Shad to day for Dinner! I had a fine Wild Turkey Hen!—Kiss our sweet littles for me. Kiss your dear Wives. Kiss each of yourselves all round for my sake, remember me to the Servants, ...and believe [me] for life your Husband, Friend, Father and that with all possible affection."

April 25th. Late in this fine, warm morning the sidewheeler *Omega* of Pierre Chouteau Jr. and Company, commanded by one of the partners, Captain Joseph A. Sire (pronounced *Sear*), casts off with its load of freight and passengers headed for the fur-company posts along the upper Missouri. As she pulls away from shore, a crowd of rough-looking drunks on her upper deck yell and fire their rifles in the air in a disorganized farewell salute. A few Indians, seated as high up on the steamer as they can find perches, solemnly watch this raucous display.

The St. Louis waterfront recedes and spreads out before them. The river is so flooded that the thicket of steamboats taking on freight at the levee almost touches the buildings of the waterfront. With her power-plant making the entire boat shudder, the *Omega* churns upstream against an eight-mile-an-hour current toward the mouth of the Missouri twenty miles away. She moves about as fast as a man can stroll. The scattered rifle salutes from the hurricane deck continue. The disreputable characters doing the shooting seem to Harris "to be the very off-scouring of the Earth, worse than any crew of sailors I ever met with." They are *engagés,* indentured to the fur company as trappers, and there are a hundred and one of them aboard, most of them French or Cana-

dian. "They are spoken to as if slaves and treated much as if such," Audubon writes in the letter home he has started today, "but the more so, the better they seem to like their employers." They will eat in gangs of ten or twelve during this trip, each gang taking its turn at a wooden trough. Audubon has been told that the standard fare poured into the trencher is a mixture of corn and fat or lard. "They sleep wherever they can lay down on skins &c, and that is the beginning of the life of a *Trapper!*"

A company official invites the Indians—Iowas, Sacs, and Foxes, headed home to their villages—to look at Audubon's sample plates of quadrupeds. "The effect was beyond belief surprising," Audubon writes. "One of the women actually ran off at the sight of the Wood Chuck exclaiming that they were alive. The chiefs knew all the animals except the

Swiss artist Karl Bodmer depicted the steamer "Yellowstone" ascending the Missouri in 1833. (Internorth Art Foundation/Joslyn Art Museum, Omaha)

Little Squirrels from the Oregon...They called me the *Great Medicine.*"

April 26th. The Missouri is over its banks in many places and yellow with mud. For a while this rainy day the current is "so Strong as to turn the Boat ashore being impossible to steer Her," reports John Bell. He shoots a Canada goose from the deck when the *Omega* is under way, and Captain Sire refuses to stop to pick it up. The captain, a handsome, imposing man, and like Audubon a French émigré, has a round trip of thirty-six hundred miles to accomplish before summer makes the Missouri too shallow to float his steamer, and there will be plenty of delays along the way as it is. But Audubon is "sorry to see the poor bird dead, uselessly."

Audubon is fifty-eight years old today. A few days ago his last remaining tooth fell out.

May 2nd. After a week the *Omega* reaches Independence, three hundred and seventy-nine miles above St. Louis. This is the traditional rendezvous point for those setting out on far-western trade and travel. Audubon notices that another steamboat is off-loading freight, and he assumes it is for the Santa Fe traders: "We saw many of their wagons." But in fact, at least some of those boxes of freight and some of those wagons are probably bound not for Mexico but for Oregon, across the Rockies. A small wagon train went there from here two summers ago, and in less than three weeks the head of the first sizable Oregon wagon train—about a thousand wagons in all—will move out.

A man can only guess at what history will find important about his era. Mostly he guesses wrong. Part of the problem is that, like Audubon at Independence in this spring of 1843, he doesn't even notice what's happening. But key events in Audubon's career have coincided precisely, or nearly so, with key events in America's great westward expansion. In 1804, the year after Audubon first arrived in the United States from France, Lewis and Clark left St. Louis to explore northwestward, up the Missouri River to its source and from there to the Pacific. Four years later, John Jacob Astor founded the American Fur Company, whose traders and trappers, along with the traders and trappers employed by competing fur companies, would rapidly (if unintentionally) open the way for settlers in the territory Lewis and Clark had explored. And at almost the same time, Audubon himself, setting up in business in Kentucky, became a part of the expansionist wave that was sweeping over the Appalachians. By 1843 the leading edge of

that wave has rolled beyond the Mississippi and is ready to start pouring toward the Rockies and the Pacific Coast.

May. The *Omega* crawls northwest along the shallow river that twists through the prairies, past Fort Leavenworth, the last permanent Army post on the river, and past the Council Bluffs. As he leaves them behind, Captain Sire ticks off in his log the names of rivers and landmarks and fur posts. They are Indian names and names of fur trappers and traders. Blacksnake Hills, Trudeau Island, Hart's Bluffs, the Big and Little Sioux, the Vermillion houses, Perkins' woods, the Iowa, the Jacques, the Bazille, the Chouteau, Bijoux Hills, John's Bluffs, the Platte, the Medicine, the Little Cheyenne. He also makes notes about the location of the Missouri's channel and the depth of the water, plus the places he stops to take on wood or might stop on his way down or during next year's voyage upriver.

On the banks, the Carolina parakeets and wild turkeys and fox squirrels dwindle and disappear as do the dense forests of sycamore, oak, hickory, beech, and maple. Now cedar and cottonwood crowd the bottoms, islands, and ravines. Audubon writes: "We have seen extensive Prairie...that have been so innundated as to have at present deposits of mud to the depth of 6 inches to 20 through which no grass can force its way this year! Glorious times this for the Geese Ducks and Gulls which are breeding all over these great plains now of mud and water puddles...The aspect of the country generally has noticeably changed with a few past days. The hills are nearly bare of timber and have no underwood or brushwood; the shores along these Hills look wilder the further we proceed, and from their tops we see nothing but miserable and interminable Prairies which we are told reach all the way to the Rocky Mountains."

The steamboat proceeds only when there is daylight enough to see by. "No one going down to New Orleans even 20 years ago can have an Idea of the Snags, Sawyers, and Planters that are found in the 'Upper Missouri,'" writes Audubon. "They show [their] brittly prongs as if some thousands of mammouth Elk Horns had been planted everywhere for the purpose of impeding the navigation." Sandbars poke across their path in unexpected places. The channel isn't charted, except by notes in Captain Sire's old logbooks and in his head, so when in doubt he sends the boat's "yawl" or tender ahead to sound for a channel—a laborious process. Even so, the *Omega* sometimes goes

aground. Then a cable is carried forward a few hundred yards by the yawl and hitched to a tree on the shore. Once the steamer has been backed off the bar, the cable keeps her heading into the current while her wheels are shifted to forward propulsion and she picks up headway. During one such crucial transition on this trip the cable breaks and she is swept broadside onto another bar and isn't hauled off until the next day. At other times the captain may have tall poles cut and brought from the woods to be planted beside the boat as part of a block-and-tackle rig that—after several poles break—lifts the *Omega* clear. As the solution of last resort, he can order the *engagés* to lighten the boat by unloading some of the cargo and carrying it around the obstruction.

High winds occasionally make the *Omega* unsteerable and force Captain Sire to tie up and wait in some sheltered place against the bank. He also has to stop frequently to have the *engagés* cut and load firewood. Once a day the boilers are washed out, because Missouri River mud collects there. Even at that, deposits of mud cause one of the boilers to burn out, and the repairs take the better part of three days.

One morning during this halt for repairs, the captain wakes Audubon at 3:45. Four mackinaw boats bound for St. Louis have come alongside—large, flat-bottomed freight scows, each with a cargo of baled buffalo robes stacked under a hood of saplings and skins that covers most of the space aboard. Their propulsion is provided by the river and by oarsmen at the bow. This is the transportation Audubon plans to use for the return voyage. He and his friends get out of bed immediately to write letters to go down to the post office at St. Louis, and the men commanding the mackinaw flotilla relay a piece of bad news. Apparently an employe at the Chouteau company's Fort McKenzie, which is just below the Falls of the Missouri, within sight of the Rockies, has killed a Blackfoot chief. So the Blackfoot country near the mountains will be an unsafe place for a party of naturalists this summer, and they will not be able to explore many miles beyond the mouth of the Yellowstone. All his life Audubon has longed to visit "the mountains of the wind," and he had high hopes he was going to see them at last.

Sometimes the stops the *Omega* is forced to make last long enough so the naturalists

can go hunting. Audubon quickly discovers that regardless of what he might have said to that reporter in St. Louis he is not up to any thirty-five-mile hikes. He tires much more easily than he expected and comments on the fact several times. He becomes cautious about overextending himself, and on mornings when he would once have been the first man out on the hunt, he waits for his breakfast instead. Bell and Squires and Harris are much more active, and they champ at the bit when they have to observe the terrain from a boat deck in the middle of the river.

When they do get ashore they find that Captain Sire's boarding bell usually rings too soon for them to collect many quadrupeds, but they do better with birds. Harris, for example, brings Audubon a large sparrow with a pink bill and black crown, face, and throat. Audubon doesn't recognize it and decides it's new. Actually, his friend Thomas Nuttall of Boston found this species years ago, a few miles west of Independence, and got around

to describing it under the name mourning finch in the second edition of his *Manual of Ornithology of the United States and Canada*, published in 1840. Audubon has attended to other pressing matters since he finished publishing the double-elephant folio and the first collection of his bird essays, and he hasn't been keeping up with all the latest discoveries of birds. He names it Harris' finch (now called Harris' sparrow).

The next day John Bell collects a small vireo, which Audubon believes (this time correctly) is a new species. We know it as Bell's vireo. Farther along, Bell notices that the meadowlark of this region doesn't sing at all like the meadowlark of the East. They collect several specimens and are puzzled because the birds look to them exactly like the eastern meadowlark. "Yet it is utterly impossible," writes Edward Harris, "that the same bird in different parts of the world can have notes so totally different." The claim of having discovered a new species will have to wait until they are home again and have access to a large collection of eastern specimens for comparison. (It is a "good" species, never formally described before. Lewis and Clark noticed it along the Missouri almost forty years earlier, but other naturalists traveling in the West after that overlooked it—just as Audubon thinks he might have if John Bell hadn't been along. The scientific name Audubon will give it is *Sturnella neglecta,* the neglected meadowlark.) Soon after pointing out the odd meadowlark song, Bell brings in a small sparrow that looks interesting to Audubon but also will have to be compared with similar skins back in New York. (It will become LeConte's sparrow, named for a young physician–naturalist who is another friend of Audubon's.)

"I Spend nearly all my time at my Journal," Audubon writes, "philosophizing as it were on all that I see and all that occurs during our slow days of progress." He takes many notes on stories he hears about the larger fur-bearing animals of the region, after checking with Captain Sire as to the reliability of the teller. Audubon and Sprague sketch and draw as the opportunity arises, but when under way the *Omega* usually shakes too badly for them to do serious work. "Squires has been engaged in making a map of the River ever since we left the Council's Bluffs and we hope that it may assist us on our return. Bell skins everything that is worth having of course . . . Harris takes notes on the Geology of the shores &c." Harris also performs the duties of boat physician, although he is not a doctor. He has been treating the *engagés,* mostly for venereal diseases, but he also takes charge when one cuts a foot badly with an ax.

Beyond Leavenworth, the land west of the river is all Indian country. Before they reach the Platte they leave the northern boundary of Missouri to the east, and "all the people we will see will be Indians, Indians, and nothing but Indians," Audubon writes. The wilderness at last.

Audubon has mixed feelings about the wilderness. After the *Omega* stops at the Blacksnake Hills settlement (today's St. Joseph, Missouri), he reports to his family that he "was delighted to see this truly beautiful site for a town or city, as will be no doubt some fifty years hence." Delighted to see the wilderness civilized? A contradiction in attitude that he shares with many of his thoughtful contemporaries. From a religious and philosophical point of view, wilderness is to Audubon the ideal condition of the Earth—fresh from the hand of God. "There is nothing perfect but *primitiveness*," he

once wrote. Primitive America is rapidly disappearing; he knows that, and he regrets it with romantic fervor. In Scotland some years ago, after he learned he was about to be introduced to the novelist Sir Walter Scott, he wrote in his journal: "Hundreds of times have I said quite loud in the woods, as I looked on a silvery streamlet or the sickly swamp or the noble Ohio, or on mountaintops losing their peaks in grey mist, Oh Walter Scott, where art thou? Wilt thou not come to my country? Wrestle with mankind and stop their increasing ravages on Nature, and describe her now for the sake of future ages. Neither this little stream, this swamp, this grand sheet of flowing water, nor these mountains will be seen in a century hence as I see them now. Nature will have been robbed of her brilliant charms . . . Oh Walter Scott, come, come to America. Get thee hence, look upon her, and see her grandeur. Nature still nurses her, cherishes her. But a tear flows in her eye. Her cheek has already changed from the peach blossom to sallow hue. Her frame inclines to emaciation. Her step is arrested. Without thee, Walter Scott, she must die, unknown to the world." Audubon was too shy to make such a suggestion to Scott when they met, but he later tried—with considerable success—to supply the Scott-like portrait of his adopted country himself.

Still, he has spent much of his life on or near the American frontier, and he greatly admires the energy and courage of the pioneers who have met and tamed the wilderness, who have been leveling the forests he loves and building farms and towns. To his mind the frontier and the wilderness can be ennobling, shaping ordinary mortals into such heroic characters as Daniel Boone.

As for "Indians, Indians, and nothing but Indians," he has mixed feelings about that, too. One afternoon the boat stops at a reservation and after the Foxes, Sacs, and Iowas disembark there, he remarks that he is glad to see them go. Many Americans of his generation are of two minds about Indians, just as they are about the wilderness. Indians in their primitiveness once seemed noble and poetic; they certainly did to Audubon. But now—tricked, corrupted, robbed, and bullied by the irresistible tide of white men, and looked upon as in the way of progress— their popular image changes. Here on the upper Missouri the trappers and fur traders mostly see them as backward, deceitful, and dangerous.

Audubon has brought with him George Catlin's *North American Indians,* published two years previously. In many respects its text

Unlike the plates for "The Birds of America," which were engraved on copper and colored by hand, drawings for "The Viviparous Quadrupeds" were printed in color by stone lithography, then finished by hand. Above are Audubon's lithograph portrait of a white wolf (National Audubon Society Library) and the stone used to make it.

and plates are a celebration of the old ideas of nobility and poetry, and the fur-company men on board have not a good word to say for it. As Audubon watches the Indians get off at the reservation he sees no signs of emotion either from them or from the Indians who meet the boat—"nothing to corroborate Mr. Catlin's views of savage life." When he learns that Indians commonly search the riverbank for the swollen, putrid carcasses of drowned buffalo—hundreds of which are seen floating downriver every spring—and cut out the hump above the shoulders for food, he exclaims in his journal, "Ah! Mr. Catlin, I am now sorry to see and to read your accounts of the Indians *you* saw—how very different they must have been from any that I have seen!"

One morning in late May a few Indians create a moment of real danger. As the *Omega* rumbles upstream with about a hundred men lounging on the deck, a small band of Indians signals from the bank that they want the boat to land for them. Captain Sire ignores them, and after the boat has

passed they begin firing at it, "not with blank cartridges," Audubon remarks in surprise, "but with well-directed rifle-balls." Four or five shots are fired, several of which hit the boat. Fortunately no one is hurt, but one ball does rip the pants of a man asleep in his bunk below, scaring him half to death.

May 23rd. A party of hunters—*"Hunters!"* exclaims Audubon derisively—was put ashore last night to shoot buffalo for food and comes aboard this morning with only about forty pounds of meat and one tongue, although four buffalo were shot. The men were too lazy to carry more of the meat. Audubon is furious: "Thus it is that thousands multiplied by thousands of Buffaloes are murdered in senseless play, and their enormous carcasses are suffered to be the prey of the Wolf, the Raven, and the Buzzard."

May 26th. In late afternoon, as the *Omega* enters the Great Bend of the Missouri, Audubon, Bell, Harris, Sprague, and three company men are landed on the west bank.

While the boat negotiates the twenty-six miles of river around the bend, they will cross the waist of the bend—a distance of two or three miles—and do some hunting. They are now in big-game country and on the lookout for buffalo, wolves, Rocky Mountain sheep, deer, elk, antelope, and bears. Walking over a broad prairie dotted with cactus, they find upland sandpipers, a long-billed curlew, and a prairie-dog town. The little marmots whistle, somersault into their holes, and outwait the hunters, who want to reach the far side of the bend before dark.

Halfway across, Audubon and his companions scramble up a steep, pebbly clay bluff, and at the top, Audubon says, have "the gratification of seeing around us one of the great panoramas this remarkable portion of our country affords." Thousands of buffalo are scattered in small groups on the plain below, and to the east are "the wanderings of the Missouri for many miles," looking at that distance like a "small, very circuitous streamlet." They descend to make camp on the far side of the bend, beside a clump of trees that

looks almost as if it might have sprung from a single set of roots. The Camp of the Six Cottonwoods, Audubon calls the place. He fixes the romantic scene in his memory—the dark night, the bright fire lighting the six cottonwoods, men bringing in wood and water and skinning and butchering a mule deer that one of the hunters has shot for supper. "Choice morceaux" of the venison, says Harris, are soon roasting on sharp sticks driven into the ground around the fire. "We all agreed it was the best Venison we ever tasted, and none failed to do ample justice to the repast." The naturalists inflate their India-rubber mattresses and roll themselves in their blankets, feet toward the fire. Isaac Sprague finds the situation "one of novelty, it being my first encampment in the open air."

June 1st. During the stop at Fort Pierre, where about half the freight and half the *engagés* are put off, Sprague asks Audubon's permission to quit the expedition and go back on the *Omega*. Audubon is "somewhat surprised . . . Of course I told him that he

Audubon wrote that wolves near Fort Union were of various colors, including gray, brindled, and white, but that white animals were by far the commonest. Earlier authors had divided North American wolves into species according to color, but the "Quadrupeds" text treated them as one, Canis lupus. *Modern mammalogists, however, consider the red wolf of Gulf states a separate species. (Curt Chapman, photographer; stone from Cincinnati Museum of Natural History)*

Overleaf: The lithograph of Audubon's buffalo painting (National Audubon Society Library).

was at liberty to do so, though it will keep me grinding about double as much as I expected." Sprague writes nothing about this in his journal, today or any day, but in a long talk with Audubon later he explains that he thought Audubon was displeased with him, "a thing that never came into my head," says Audubon, "and in all probability he will remain with us."

June 6th. They meet another flotilla of four company mackinaw boats, coming down from the post at the Falls of the Missouri. It is manned by "a peculiar looking crew," says Audubon, "who appeared not much better than a set of bandits among the Pyranees or the Alps; yet they seem to be the very best sort of men for trappers and boatmen." "They confirm the report," adds Harris, "that one of their Clerks . . . shot a Blackfoot Chief. They say that the traders are obliged to confine themselves to the fort, and that only five of the Blackfeet are admitted at a time to trade. This state of affairs will prevent our visiting that interesting region."

June 7th. On a cold and rainy morning, wind in the northeast, the *Omega* pulls into the bank at the fur company's Fort Clark and the "Mandan Village." The Mandans, a settled, agricultural tribe, no longer live in their large dome-like lodges of cottonwood timbers and earth. In fact, the Mandans scarcely exist at all. In the spring of 1837 a fur-company steamboat, prophetically called the *St. Peter,* brought smallpox up the river, starting an epidemic that killed thousands of Indians between the Missouri and the mountains. It reduced a community of an estimated sixteen hundred Mandans to a remnant of about a hundred, and they fled their village, which is now occupied by some of their relatives, the Arikaras. "As soon as we were near the shore," says Audubon, "every article that could conveniently be carried off was placed under lock and key . . . The appearance of these poor, miserable devils, as we approached the shore, was wretched enough. There they stood in the pelting rain and keen wind, covered with Buffalo robes, red blankets, and the like, some partially and most curiously besmeared with mud; and as they came on board, and we shook hands with each of them, I felt a clamminess that rendered the ceremony most repulsive.... They all looked very poor; and our captain says they are the *ne plus ultra* of thieves." As the consignment of freight for Fort Clark is put ashore, Audubon and Harris play tourist and are guided through the muddy village. In a journal entry at day's end Audubon remarks that "it will indeed be a deliverance to get rid of all this 'Indian poetry.'" Isaac Sprague expresses the same thought: "A visit to their village such a day as this destroys all the romance of Indian life."

June 9th. While they are stopped to take on firewood, a buffalo cow swims across the river upstream of the boat. As she struggles to climb the steep bank, one of the company men shoots her, jumps on her back, and yells for a rope, to keep her from floating away. A line is tossed to him, and with the dead buffalo safely tethered he and she drift down to the *Omega* side by side, where she is hauled up on deck. Audubon and Sprague quickly measure her: from nose to root of tail, eight feet; from the top of the foreshoulder to the hoof, four feet nine and one-half inches; from the top of the rump to the hoof, four feet two inches. Then she is butchered with all the dispatch, says Edward Harris, of "a hog killing in Cincinnati," and with some fur-country elaborations. He and Audubon watch—fascinated but queasy—as two Indians take out the cow's manifold or third stomach, empty it, dip it in blood, eat it, then repeat the same process with the udder. The fur-company men say those parts are delicious eaten raw. Harris won't test the assertion, but Audubon, always willing to try a new taste, accepts a well-washed piece of the stomach and is astonished to find it "very good," though the idea still repels him. He has been given the intact cow's head to draw; otherwise he and his friends would see another demonstration that would shock them more: Indians and veteran trappers alike are partial to raw buffalo brains.

June 12th. Late in the day the *Omega* passes the mouth of the Yellowstone. At sunset, when she arrives at Fort Union, six and one-half miles beyond, cannons roar and flags are hoisted on the steamer and on the fort. The boat has made the trip in less than forty-nine days, cutting fifteen days from the previous record. The bourgeois, or boss of the fort, Alexander Culbertson, rides down with his men—in "quite a cavalcade," notes Audubon—to greet Captain Sire and his guests,

and invites them to join him for a glass of port wine. They walk up to the fort. It stands about seventy-five yards from the Missouri on a plain that reaches back a mile and one-half to the feet of high bluffs at the edge of a curious and forbidding terrain—where prairie is cut by mazes of deep ravines and badland gulches.

This new base of operations for Audubon and company is a fort in fact as well as in name. Twenty-foot-high walls of cottonwood pickets, their feet in a stone foundation, form a rectangle two hundred twenty by two hundred forty feet. Two massive stone towers more than thirty feet high stand at the northeast and southwest corners, each sprouting a balcony from which to overlook the countryside. They are stocked with light artillery and small arms, ready for a fight. A gallery runs all around the inside of the fort, five feet below the tops of the picket walls, for the sake of defense and observation. The front gate is doubled in such a way that parties of Indians can be allowed in to trade or parley without actually entering the fort proper.

All the buildings of the community back up to the walls within the fort: living quarters for Culbertson and his young Blackfoot wife, Natawista, and their baby; quarters for the clerks of the fort and for guests; a tailor's shop, retail store, warehouse, and various storerooms, including a "press room" for furs big enough to hold up to 30,000 buffalo robes. There are also dormitories for the company's hunters and other employes, an icehouse filled with river ice, a cook-house, stables for horses, cattle, and buffalo calves, a henhouse, dairy, cooper's shop, a combination blacksmith–gunsmith–tinner's shop, a coal-house, and a heavily built powder magazine.

These structures surround an open parade ground or yard, at the middle of which is a small vegetable garden and a four-pounder iron cannon. In the middle of the little garden is a sixty-three-foot flagpole, "the glory of the fort," according to its chief clerk, Edward Denig, "for on high, seen from far and wide, floats the Star Spangled Banner, an immense flag which once belonged to the United States Navy, and gives the certainty of security from dangers, rest to the weary traveller, peace and plenty to the fatigued and hungry, whose eyes are gladdened by the sight of it on arriving from the long and perilous voyages usual in this far western wild."

Early the next morning Audubon writes a letter home in which he is breathless with excitement: "We have seen an immensity of Game of all description [on the way]. Yester-

Fort Union pictured at left by Karl Bodmer. (Courtesy of Internorth Art Foundation/Joslyn Art Museum).

day and within only 3 miles of this place, we saw 22 Mountain Rams in one flock, and saw them for nearly 10 minutes running up and down Hills as if so many unaccountably active Sheep. Grisley Bears are abundant too, and Wolves are not to be [counted] . . . My head is so full that I cannot find matter scarcely to write a letter . . . My head is actually swimming with excitement and I cannot write any more."

That letter goes downriver aboard the *Omega,* along with a copy of Audubon's journal to this point, a bundle of skins, and a modest collection of specimens preserved on the up-voyage. There are more than ten dozen bird skins but only about a dozen mammals, including a few rabbits and a hare, two groundhogs, three wood rats. A few more mammal specimens are in barrels of pickle—the head and two feet of the buffalo cow, a buffalo calf, and head and feet of a wolf. They will travel down the river with the expedition late in the summer.

Audubon plans to start back about August 15th or 20th. That will allow them enough time to "go down very leisurely" before the cold weather and snow set in on the Plains, so they can then explore places they couldn't on the way up. That plan gives them two months at Fort Union.

Midsummer. The people of the fort are every bit as excited to see the newcomers as Audubon is to be there. For the most part since last fall they have seen only the men at Fort Mortimer, the "opposition" trading post a few miles below, and occasional groups of Indians who have come to trade and camp outside the walls. While Audubon and his friends watch from the balcony below the tops of the pickets, Alexander Culbertson and two of his men put on a small Wild West show in the prairie behind the fort. First there is a chase on horseback after an unlucky wolf that happened to appear on the scene. Then Culbertson gives a no-hands riding demonstration, guiding his horse with only his body, as he would when loading a rifle in mid-chase. He and the other riders follow this with a mock buffalo hunt—real ammunition but no buffalo—loading and firing their guns repeatedly as they race down out of the hills toward the fort at a full gallop. That evening a dance is held in Culbertson's house, music provided by clarinet, fiddle, and drum, and the trappers and clerks swing their Indian women through cotillions and reels until one o'clock in the morning.

Audubon attacks his assignment at Fort Union in several ways. He makes it known that he will buy animals, dead or alive, in

good condition, and on occasion he offers specific rewards for certain animals. He and his companions will hunt, of course. Since they are newcomers, the fur company has assigned one of its veteran hunters, Etienne Provost, who has been in fur country for twenty years, to assist them. The bourgeois at Fort Pierre has provided them with a second hunter, and Alexander Culbertson also makes available a few of his most reliable men at Fort Union. These hunters and Audubon's friends go out in various directions, in parties of two or more for safety, on an almost daily basis. Audubon also enlists the help of the "opposition" at Fort Mortimer, and the hunters there sometimes make forays on his behalf.

Audubon's own hunting remains limited. He will not join a hunt for bighorns, for example, because "I, alas! am no longer young and alert enough for the expedition." When he rides, his mount is an old plug that "stands gunfire like a stump." He has trouble with his feet, too. They are stabbed by cactus and blistered by walking, and halfway through the visit at Fort Union he reports they are very sore. His dwindling stamina even affects his drawing. "I began drawing at five this morning," he writes on the last day of June, "and worked almost without cessa-

tion till after three, when, becoming fatigued . . . I took a short walk, regretting I could no longer draw twelve or fourteen hours without a pause or thought of weariness."

But the first four weeks of the visit are full of activity and success, and Audubon and Isaac Sprague are kept busy drawing animals and plants—and painting portraits of Mr. and Mrs. Culbertson. Almost immediately the naturalists run into a fascinating puzzle concerning flickers. They are in a region where the ranges of several very closely related birds overlap, including the indigo and lazuli buntings, the two meadowlarks, and members of the red-tailed hawk group. Some of these birds not only meet but also mix. Audubon's engravings and his *Ornithological Biography* include depictions and descriptions of the red-shafted flicker of the West and the yellow-shafted flicker of the East, known to Audubon and his contemporaries by the names red-shafted woodpecker and golden-winged or golden-shafted woodpecker. Both are seen around Fort Union. After less than a week, Bell and Harris come in from a hunt carrying a male yellow-shafted flicker that has a red mark on the cheek instead of a black one. Within a few days they and Sprague collect enough females and unfledged young with similar

Son John W. also painted the original of the "Long-tailed Deer" which, despite some doubts, John Bachman decided to rank as a separate species. It was only a variety of the white-tailed deer. (National Audubon Society Library)

*Drawings for the litho-
graphs of the striped
skunk were the senior
Audubon's work.
(National Audubon
Society Library)*

markings for Audubon to declare that they have found a new species, which he calls the Missouri red-moustached woodpecker. Then they begin to find more kinds of "new" flickers, birds with gradations and combinations of the colors and markings of red-shafts and yellow-shafts. One afternoon Harris and Sprague bring Audubon five flicker specimens of four different types, and he calls them "the most curious set of five birds I ever saw . . . which I think will puzzle all the naturalists in the world." (He will later publish his red-moustached woodpecker as a third flicker species—and be wrong, but ornithologists will take more than a century to solve the puzzle by deciding that red-shafts and yellow-shafts and all flickers in between are one species.)

There's also a puzzle with the local white-tailed deer, the commonest big mammal around the fort. Does are easy to collect in the spring when the fawns are still dependent on them—or at least the fur-country hunters make them easy to collect. Provost is a skilled manufacturer of a whistle he calls "the bleater." Blow on it, and any doe within hearing runs to the spot, believing her fawn is in trouble. Audubon calls this "a cruel, deceitful, and unsportsmanlike method" and tries to discourage the practice, but even his own companions ignore him. And it does produce specimens. Harris soon notices that the tails of these deer are considerably longer than those of eastern whitetails. The animals also are bigger, and Bell thinks he sees some differences from the eastern whitetail in the deer's actions when running—all of which fit Lewis and Clark's reports of a "long-tailed" deer in the region. So in an effort to establish the distinction—which ultimately they fail to do—they collect a good many skins of big whitetail does.

As the hot weather begins to take hold, the returns from the hunts diminish rapidly. The game Audubon thought was so abundant when he arrived often proves frustratingly difficult to acquire. Fur traders have lived year-round at the confluence of the Missouri and the Yellowstone since the autumn of 1828, and the area has been well hunted over. In fact, all the fur country south of Canada, from the Missouri up into the Rockies, has been hunted and trapped hard for nearly forty years, with no one giving much thought to the future. There aren't many fur-bearing animals of commercial value left.

Furthermore, mammals, particularly the small species, are just plain elusive. There is, for example, a small hare, said to be very common in the vicinity. During the first week at Fort Union, John Bell brings in a badly damaged specimen of the animal, but enough of it so that Audubon believes it represents a new species. It becomes the object of repeated and unsuccessful hunts.

In daylight the hares seem to stay mostly in the shelter of dense, often thorny shrubs—especially when under siege—and not even Harris' pointer, Brag, can flush them from cover. One afternoon Harris goes out alone for another try. He finds no hares in the open, but on the side of a ravine, about an hour's walk from the fort, he locates a clump of bushes that he believes contains some of them. A short while before sunset he sits down on a facing bank to wait for them to appear. By nine o'clock he still has not seen a sign of them, and as he gives up the vigil he stops beside the bushes to listen. He is positive he can hear the hares rustling about.

At Fort Union an hour later, Culbertson scolds Harris sternly. It was very dangerous to go so far alone, he says, and Harris must not try it again.

Hunting mammals for science on the prairies of the upper Missouri can be time-consuming in other ways as well. Once a large specimen is tracked down and shot, the hunter must immediately see to its preservation. One of the company hunters shoots two antelope for Audubon. He's within a few miles of the fort and stands a chance of bringing the animals in whole, but to do so he must leave them on the prairie and go fetch a mule and cart to haul them. But wolves are attracted to gunfire and may well destroy the specimens while he's gone. The hunters of the fur country use a trick they say protects their take from wolves: They drape an article of clothing—even a handkerchief will do—on each carcass. Sometimes it works, sometimes not. If not, a long hunt is made worthless.

Audubon and his friends do very well with birds, which are relatively easy to collect, carry, and preserve. Among them is a new pipit, named after Isaac Sprague, who finds the nest and eggs and collects the first specimen of the female. Another is a new sparrow, which Audubon names for his young friend Spencer Baird. Audubon writes detailed descriptions of animal behavior—what he and his colleagues observe as well as observations made by habitués of the fur country. He writes up dozens of fur-country anecdotes, which Bachman can weave into his texts about the western animals. He solicits contributions to his journal from officials at the fort. But by the middle of the summer he still lacks many animals of which he wants

PLATE XLII.

Drawn from Nature by J. J. Audubon, F.R.S. F.L.S.

Lith. Printed & Col.d by J. T. Bowen, Philad.a 1843.

MEPHITIS AMERICANA, DESM.

COMMON AMERICAN SKUNK

Natural size

FEMALE.

drawings, and his specimen collection of quadrupeds is even more disappointing.

As Harris notes in mid-July, "the ground within walking distance of the Fort is pretty well used up for new or rare birds or quadrupeds and the walking distance is very much circumscribed by the excessive heat." Provost and other company hunters lead trips farther afield, but with strikingly thin results. Culbertson tries to help by organizing two- and three-day hunts for the Audubon party, which take them out into new terrain. But these coincide with the appearance of buffalo herds, and they turn into wild, competitive buffalo hunts.

On a hot day in late July, Audubon and a few of the company hunters gather on a hilltop to watch a chase after four buffalo. Below them, Harris, Squires, Bell, and Culbertson, guns loaded, begin their approach to the buffalo under the cover of the hill, then ride forward in single file, to appear like one horseman, not four. When they are within two hundred yards, the bulls break into a run, two going in one direction, two in another. The hunters have agreed to shoot at only one animal apiece so each man may have his own buffalo at the end. Harris and Squires wheel to one side after one pair, and Squires takes the first shot. His bull, hit, turns on him, and Squires' horse shies to avoid a charge. Squires is thrown ten feet over the horse's neck and is hurt landing on his own powderhorn. But he is up in an instant, chasing his horse on foot while the bull runs away. Harris races on and with his second shot kills his bull; then he gallops after Squires' horse. Meanwhile the two animals Bell and Culbertson have followed run "round and round a small hill like circus horses four times," writes Bell later, "and much faster than I had any idea of, and so close together that we could not part them." At last Bell manages to turn them enough so that Culbertson and he each get two shots, and Culbertson's second ball is fatal. His bull walks slowly in Audubon's direction and collapses about sixty yards away. John Bell's quarry is still running, however, and both men reload on the fly as they chase it. Culbertson takes a shot—thereby breaking the original agreement—and Bell angrily yells him off, catches up to the bull, and kills it. Harris has caught Squires' horse and returned it to him, and they gallop after Squires' bull, but Squires, feeling the effects of his fall, is forced to give up, and the animal runs off.

The thunderous, dangerous, high-speed hunt is over, but the hunters' blood is up. They have killed more meat than they can eat or than their two carts can carry back to Fort Union. Yet that evening, when they see another small band of buffalo, they chase and kill three more while Audubon again looks on. Bell and Harris, who each bring down another large, fat animal, now cut out only the tongues and the tails—the tails are trophies—and ride back to camp regretting, writes Harris, that they have "destroyed these noble beasts for no earthly reason but to gratify a sanguinary disposition which appears to be inherent in our natures... completely disgusted with ourselves and with the conduct of all white men who come to this country."

A certain tension becomes evident between the eastern sportsmen–naturalists and the men of the fur trade. One "established rule of this country," remarks Squires in a passage he contributes to Audubon's journal, "is, 'When you can, take the best.'" That is to say, if you get to a freshly shot buffalo first, quickly cut out the best parts for yourself, regardless of who shot it. None of this high-flown after-you-my-dear-sir citified politeness. Grab it and git. And if you make a deal about who shoots what in a buffalo hunt, you don't take that seriously once the action has begun.

Squires, Harris, and Bell are addicted to buffalo hunts—"races," s Bell calls them—and can't get enough of them. But there's a bitter edge to the experience, so little sportsmanship to match the sport and such savagery around the huge carcass. After one hunt, Bell writes in his journal about the carts full of buffalo meat rolling into camp: "As soon as the carts arrived some of the men cut off pieces of liver and threw it in the fire to roast which it soon did and they took it out and commenced eating it as though it had been cooked in the very best manner and that is not half as disgusting to me as to see them eat it raw. I have seen them cut off pieces as large as my hand as soon as it was taken out of the animal and eat it and the blood running down the sides of their mouths, and I have seen them... cut open

the skull and marrow bones and eat it raw, while it is still warm from the animal. This I have seen at every Buffaloe that I have seen skinned and cut up."

Audubon is so upset by the sheer waste of the buffalo hunts that he makes an issue of it—the killing of many animals just for fun, not for food, and calls it a "terrible destruction of life... The prairies are literally *covered* with the skulls of the victims." Toward the end of his stay, Culbertson at least humors him: "My remonstrances about useless slaughter have not been wholly unheeded," remarks Audubon.

Naturally the critical attitudes flow in both directions. "When Bell was fixing his [gear] on his horse this morning," Audubon writes in early August, having just watched his assistant depart on a bighorn hunt with Provost and another company man, La Fleur, "I was amused to see Provost and La Fleur laughing outright at him, as he first put on a Buffalo robe under his saddle, a blanket over it, and over that his mosquito bar and his rain protector. These old hunters could not understand why he needed all these things to be comfortable... he [also] took a sack of ship-biscuit. Provost took only an old blanket, a few pounds of dried meat, and his tin cup, and rode off in his shirt and dirty breeches. La Fleur was worse off still, for he took no blanket, and said he could borrow Provost's tin cup."

That bighorn hunt proves, typically, unsuccessful. Audubon, although he has had many experienced hunters working for him, has managed to procure only two bighorn specimens in two months, both of them females.

By now, the timber for his mackinaw boat has been hauled to the boat-building yard, and the boat is launched August 12th. The *Union*, as he calls it, is forty feet long and eight feet broad; Audubon thinks it will prove too small. The packing begins: the many fur-country mementos they have been given, such as the necklace of grizzly claws and the elkhorn bow and the superb Indian costumes; the plants and seeds, the pieces of petrified wood, the fossils, two Indian skulls, one snake specimen; the journals and drawings; the preserved skins and skulls of about fifty quadrupeds, representing only a handful of species, many in barrels of brine; fewer than two hundred bird skins; a live badger; all their baggage and hunting gear.

Audubon regrets having promised his family that he would be home in the fall. He would like to stay at Fort Union over the winter, or so he says. But he is not staying. Perhaps he will fill some of the large gaps in the

The marsupial opossum, noted the "Quadrupeds" text, must have astounded the first Europeans to see it. Here is an animal that looks faintly like a small, hairy pig—yet sometimes hangs from a branch by its tail like a monkey, while a dozen young sit on its back, tethered to its tail by their own tails. If a stranger touches it, "instantly it seems to be struck with some mortal disease: its eyes close, it falls to the ground... and appears to be dead! He turns it on its back, and perceives on its stomach a strange apparently artificial opening... and lo! [inside] another brood of a dozen or more young, scarcely larger than a pea, are hanging in clusters." (National Audubon Society Library)

Overleaf: The lithograph of Audubon's beaver drawing from "The Viviparous Quadrupeds of North America" (National Audubon Society Library).

collection on the way downriver. Provost will act as guide and will help with the collecting, and Culbertson is coming, too, as far as company headquarters at Fort Pierre. Audubon hires an extra hunter, whom he agrees to pay by the piece: for each bighorn male, $10; for a large grizzly, $20; for a large bull elk, $6; for mule deer, either sex, $6 each; for red or small gray foxes, $3; for badgers and large porcupines, $2.

August 17th. Downward bound one day. Sprague has been very reticent in his journalizing all summer, and almost monosyllabic recently, but now he bursts with enthusiasm. "Fine day. Very pleasant on calm still days floating along this wilderness, especially in those places where the banks...are overhung by the ancient forest. Occasionally the boatmen strike up one of their wild Canadian boat songs, keeping time as they row."

August 21st. They have passed through thousands of buffalo, and Audubon has tried to capture in the pages of his leatherbound pocket diary the sound the huge bulls make, roaring in concert: "Just like the long-continued roll of 100ds of Drums... resembles the grunting of Hogs, with a rolling sound from the throat that...is heard for miles. They bellow with the head down, tearing the Earth up probably the while."

August 28th. The wind has blown a gale

all night and is still high this morning. Even when propelled by both current and oarsmen, a mackinaw boat cannot make headway against a strong wind or steer across it. So the men are often stopped, and they use the halts for hunting. The first men out today return with reports of bear tracks. A few days ago the first grizzly was collected, a young male, but Audubon needs more specimens than that, so he and three companions start after bears. "Such a walk I do not remember," Audubon scribbles in his journal. "It was awfull, Mire, Willows, Vines, &c &c &c, we returned much fatigued and having seen nothing."

September 5th. All summer long Etienne Provost, who knows as much about trapping as any man alive, has tried without success to catch a beaver for Audubon, in streams where the beaver was once abundant. Yesterday he found beaver tracks and set a couple of traps, but caught no beavers. This morning at dawn the traps are still empty. Audubon has to be satisfied with two large pieces of saplings beavers have cut down, a pocketful of their wood chips, and a look at the inside of the beaver lodge, which the men tear apart for examination.

September 7th. While they are windbound this morning and consequently out hunting, a whip-poor-will flushes from the ground in front of Bell and drops back into cover. When it flushes a second time he realizes that it is a good deal smaller than the common whip-poor-will of the East, and he shoots it. "I have no doubt," writes Audubon delightedly after studying the specimen, "[it] is the one found on the Rocky Mountains by Nuttall." That was nine years ago, and Nuttall only *saw* it and didn't bring home any specimens, though he mentioned it to Audubon. So it has not yet been officially discovered. Audubon promptly names it *Caprimulgus nuttallii,* Nuttall's whip-poor-will (now called poor-will). That night at about ten o'clock, "Harris called me to hear the notes of the new Whippoorwill. We heard 2 at once and the sound was thus *Oh-will!* repeated often and quickly as in our common species." It is the last new bird species Audubon will play a part in discovering.

September 14th. At Fort Pierre they have exchanged the *Union* for a larger mackinaw boat and have reloaded, with more room now for the collection—which includes the live kit fox Audubon was given at the Mandan Village—and for the many souvenirs they have gathered at Fort Pierre. Nine miles below the fort they stop at the fort's farm and buy a pig, some potatoes, and corn. After a month of eating off the land, these luxuries are hints of civilization, though they will be on the river—slowed by winds and storms and sandbars—five weeks longer.

October 8th. They push off from camp early in this cold and rainy morning but are forced to halt twice because of the wind. They play cards to fill the time. Whenever the wind diminishes enough, they drift and row a few more miles, but when it revives in the late afternoon they give up and stop to make camp. This is their second night in the state of Missouri, notes Bell, "& we now see a great number of log cabins all along the shore where there is a good place. This is on the left. On the right is still the Indian Country. The People here raise plenty of Corn & Potatoes for their own use, & gather great quantities of Honey which they find in the woods." The naturalists now have a few dragoons on board whom they are giving a ride down to Fort Leavenworth, and Au-

Like the engravings of birds in the Double Elephant Folio, the "Quadrupeds" lithographs showed animals in characteristic activity and often included domestic settings as background. The black-footed ferret is the work of John Woodhouse Audubon. His father never found or heard of the ferret when he was in fur country; it has always been an elusive creature. But a specimen reached him later through John Bell, and Audubon and Bachman were the first to describe the species. (National Audubon Society Library)

PLATE XCIII

PUTORIUS NIGRIPES, AUD & BACH.
BLACK FOOTED FERRET.

PLATE CXLVIII.

dubon makes a present to the officer in charge of the troop—one of his sample quadrupeds plates. In return, the officer promises him a "fine black bear skin and a set of Elk Horns."

October 21st. In St. Louis the collection is packed and labeled for shipment back East. Including the mere three dozen or so specimens of birds and mammals added on the two-month down-voyage, it is strikingly small for a seven-month expedition into what was supposed to be a terrain rich in North American wildlife: five hundred specimens at most, about eighty percent of them birds. The living menagerie includes a fawn, the badger, and the kit fox, and new boxes have been built to hold them on the rest of the journey to Minnie's Land.

October 22nd–November 4th. Edward Harris will go down to New Orleans from here, but the others in the party board the steamer *Nautilus* for Cincinnati. Audubon notes this in a single sentence in his journal, his last entry of the trip. The boat casts off from the levee early in the afternoon. And as it churns down the Mississippi toward the mouth of the Ohio, Audubon, at the end of his final expedition, starts a journey backward through his life.

Much of his best work as an artist was done within sight or within an easy walk of this great silver-blue snake of a river. Some drawings were even made on a flatboat floating down toward New Orleans. That was more than twenty years ago, on his first expedition as an artist–naturalist.

After a day the *Nautilus* turns up the Ohio, and Audubon has on his left a shore where he and his elder son Victor, then fourteen years old, tramped one October twenty years ago—two hundred fifty miles from the mouth of the Ohio to Louisville. The river was too low that fall to carry steamboats. Victor was on his way to be apprenticed to an uncle, and Audubon would continue east, to Philadelphia, to see whether someone might want to publish his bird drawings. No one did.

On a rainy afternoon, the boat stops briefly at Henderson, Kentucky. He and Lucy and the boys lived here for eight years when Audubon was still a merchant and frontier entrepreneur who drew birds only as a hobby. "This Place saw My best days, My Happiest," Audubon wrote years ago in a memoir for his sons, "My wife having blessed me with . . . Woodhouse [John Woodhouse, the younger son] and a sweet Daughter I Calculated . . . to Live and [die] in Comfort, Our Business Was good of course . . . but

I was intended to meet Many Events of a Disagreable Nature...the Building of a Large Steam Mill, the Purchasing of Too Many goods sold on Credit." The collapse of Kentucky banks and businesses in 1819 took Audubon down with it, "put all to an end; the Loss of my Darling Daughter affected Me Much; My Wife apparently had Lost her spirits. I felt no wish to try the Mercantile Business. I paid all I could and Left Henderson, Poor & Miserable of thoughts." The steam-mill in which he invested so much of his time and money, and which helped bankrupt him, is still standing on the riverbank these twenty-four years later—bittersweet symbol of what drove him into a career as a world-famous artist, scientist, and man of letters.

It all reels up so fast. Now here's Shippingport and Louisville, at the Falls of the Ohio, where in 1807 he opened his first business and where Lucy and he began their married life as boarders in a riverfront hotel called the Indian Queen. In those days the falls, a long set of rocky rapids, effectively blocked much of the river traffic, so the pair of communities at either end of the rapids on the Kentucky side—Louisville upstream, Shippingport down—became prosperous ports. Downbound boats took on pilots to navigate the falls, and upbound goods and travelers were carried around them. Now a canal has been completed to bypass the falls, and the *Nautilus* negotiates it in two hours.

In Cincinnati, where they change steamers, half an inch of snow sticks to the bright-leaved trees. Audubon lived here for a few months in 1820, when he was employed as a taxidermist and artist by the Western Museum. The museum soon went broke, but the job gave him a chance to think about an idea he had—to make and publish a complete collection of life-sized drawings of North American birds. The people he worked with during those few months encouraged him to undertake the project, and when the museum folded it was from here he set out on that first purposeful birding and drawing expedition, down the Ohio and the Mississippi to New Orleans—frightened, but full of passion and hope.

They board a canal boat at Pittsburgh—a canal boat in which to cross the Alleghenies! In his twenties and thirties he rode horses over them often on business trips, exploring for birds along the way. Now he will mount and descend, one after another, via short stretches of water held in place by canal locks, and—at the top of the mountains—over a series of inclined planes with stationary steam engines. Restless, he gets out and walks a lot during this journey. A young admirer who often walks with him is struck by Audubon's conversation, "impulsive and fragmentary," marked by extended silences.

Audubon arrived home at Minnie's Land the first week of November 1843. The expedition to the Yellowstone had been a disappointment in many ways, but that was to prove all of a piece with the quadrupeds project and the remaining seven years of Audubon's life. He did the drawings of the new western birds for the octavo edition of *The Birds of America* and then went back to selling his productions and drawing plates for the work on quadrupeds. But his horizons now shrank, and rather rapidly, to the boundaries of Minnie's Land. John Bachman, struggling with the text, shouted at him by mail from Charleston, and shouted at the boys too, begging for information, books, Audubon's Missouri River journal—and got so little response that he turned to Edward Harris for help getting the material he needed. The Audubons were cranking out quadrupeds plates as fast as they could. They needed the income, and the text could wait.

By early 1846 Audubon's sight had failed to the point where he was no longer good at drawing small animals, and his son John became in effect chief artist. Less than a year later, the white-haired patriarch wrote his last letters. In one of them he recommended Spencer Baird for a curatorship in the recently established Smithsonian Institution. Sometime before the spring of 1847, before his sixty-second birthday, he began slipping out of touch with his surroundings. The cause was probably premature senile dementia, or Alzheimer's disease, perhaps complicated by a stroke. In any case, the engine that propelled the Audubon family and the quadrupeds project ran down and stopped.

To be sure, the work was finished, under the jumbled leadership of Bachman and the two Audubon sons—the plates in 1848 and the text in 1854. Many of the plates in *The Viviparous Quadrupeds* (about half the originals were painted by John Woodhouse Audubon) were every bit as good as the bird plates, and the text was colorful and lively when it had to do with species Audubon and Bachman had known firsthand. But it was incomplete and poorly organized. And unlike Audubon's works on birds it was immediately eclipsed by another publication, Spencer Fullerton Baird's *Mammals of North America,* published between 1853 and 1856 by the federal government as part of its surveys of potential routes for railroad lines across the American West.

A long-tailed weasel by John Woodhouse Audubon (National Audubon Society Library).

SOURCES

Audubon's Missouri River expedition is remarkably well documented. Chief among the sources are six sets of records, each representing major segments of the adventure. Audubon himself always kept a journal when he was on an expedition (and also through much of the rest of his life). Very few of the original manuscripts of his journals, however, still exist. Some apparently were lost or burned by accident. Others were burned on purpose by his granddaughter Maria Audubon, after she had written her own expurgated versions for publication in 1897 in "Audubon and his Journals" (Charles Scribner's Sons; Dover, 1960). The Missouri River trip of 1843 is described in one of these "Maria journals." But a fragment of the original, covering two months of the trip, also survives and is in the possession of an Audubon descendant, who generously allowed me to read it. By comparing it with the published journal, one can see the kinds of changes Maria made, some of them outrageous. Her version of what Audubon wrote remains a useful source but must be quoted cautiously and double-checked against other sources whenever possible.

Fortunately a number of letters written by Audubon during the first two months of the expedition also exist, most of them in the possession of National Audubon Society. A collection of these letters was compiled and edited by John Francis McDermott, "Audubon in the West" (University of Oklahoma Press, 1965). In addition, at least three of Audubon's four companions on the expedition, Edward Harris, Isaac Sprague, and John Bell, kept journals of the trip. One of these journals has been published: "Up the Missouri with Audubon: The Journal of Edward Harris," edited by John Francis McDermott (University of Oklahoma Press, 1951). Sprague's manuscript journal is in the collection of the Boston Athenaeum. The whereabouts of Bell's journal seems to have been unknown to historians and Audubon biographers for the last 142 years, but it miraculously turned up for me during my research for this article. It is in the possession of William Reese, a New Haven, Connecticut, rare-book dealer who kindly made the journal available for study and quotation.

Finally, the captain's log of the steamboat that carried Audubon and his party up the Missouri also survives, in French, and a translation was published in Hiram M. Chittenden's "History of Early Steamboat Navigation on the Missouri River: Life and Adventures of Joseph La Barge" (Ross & Haines, 1962).—M.H.

Previous page: John Woodhouse Audubon painted this portrait of his father a few days after the naturalist returned to New York City from the West. That done, John James Audubon, as he always did after an expedition, shaved off the mustache and beard. (American Museum of Natural History)